DR. EDWARD TAUB'S

SEVEN STEPS
TO
SELF-HEALING

DR. EDWARD TAUB'S

SEVEN STEPS TO SELF-HEALING

QUESTIONNAIRES PREPARED IN CONSULTATION WITH
RICHARD FRIEDMAN, PH.D.

Director of Research, Mind/Body Medical Institute, Harvard Medical School
and Professor of Psychiatry and Behavioral Science,
State University of New York, Stony Brook

A DK PUBLISHING BOOK

To Sathya Sai Baba, for Anneli

IMPORTANT NOTICE

This is not a medical reference book. The information it contains is general, not specific to any individual or group. The opinions expressed are those of the author and reflect his personal philosophy and beliefs. The *Seven Steps to Self-Healing* supports both traditional and nontraditional medical care but is not intended to replace specific treatments.

The author and publisher acknowledge the valuable contributions of Dr. Richard Friedman, Director of Research, Mind/Body Medical Institute, Harvard Medical School and Professor of Psychiatry and Behavioral Science, State University of New York, Stony Brook, and his assistant, Patti Myers.

Project Editor:	GILLIAN ROBERTS
Project Art Editor:	WILLIAM MASON
Senior Managing Editor:	MARY-CLARE JERRAM
Managing Art Editor:	AMANDA LUNN
Production:	MICHELLE THOMAS
US Editor:	CONSTANCE M. ROBINSON

First American Edition, 1996

2 4 6 8 10 9 7 5 3 1

Published in the United States by DK Publishing, Inc., 95 Madison Avenue, New York, NY 10016

Visit us on the World Wide Web at http://www.dk.com

Library of Congress Cataloging-in-Publication Data

Taub, Edward A.
    Seven steps to self-healing / by Edward Taub. – – 1st American ed.
      p.   cm.
    Includes index.
    ISBN 0–7894–1082–6
    1. Mind and body.   2. Mental healing.   3. Satisfaction
4. Self-help techniques   I. Title
BF161.T196   1996
158'.1– –dc20

96–7819
CIP

Text film output by The Right Type, Great Britain
Reproduced by DSI Technologies (UK) Limited, Great Britain
Printed in Hong Kong by Wing King Tong Co. Ltd

CONTENTS

FOREWORD

WESTERN MEDICINE IS BASED ALMOST EXCLUSIVELY ON REPAIRING THE HUMAN BODY RATHER THAN STIMULATING THE WILL TO BE WELL. IT HAS FORGOTTEN THAT HEALTH IS A MATTER OF BALANCING OUR PHYSICAL, MENTAL, AND SPIRITUAL ENERGIES. MY WELLNESS TREATMENT – WHICH I OFFER YOU IN SEVEN STEPS TO SELF-HEALING – EVOLVED DURING MY CAREER AS A FAMILY PHYSICIAN, PEDIATRICIAN, AND MEDICAL SCHOOL PROFESSOR. IT IS DESIGNED TO CREATE BALANCE BY STIMULATING YOUR HEALING FORCE – BY REVIVING YOUR INNATE ABILITY TO HEAL YOURSELF.

YOUR HEALING FORCE CAN OVERCOME ILLNESS, CONQUER ADDICTIONS, AND REVERSE STRESS. UNLEASHING ITS POWER CAN BRING WONDERFUL BENEFITS. OUR HEALTH CARE SYSTEMS MAY BE FLAWED, BUT THE NOBILITY OF MEDICINE REMAINS. I WOULD BE HONORED TO SERVE AS YOUR GUIDE AND WELLNESS PHYSICIAN AS YOU TRAVEL THE PATH TO SELF-HEALING.

THE HEALI

NG FORCE

ILLNESS BEGINS IN THE MIND

The mind is the entity within each human organism that regulates and controls all of its systems. Whatever the system – metabolic, nervous, hormonal, cardiovascular, reproductive, digestive, renal, circulatory – each one is capable of perfect interaction with every other to produce the whole range of emotions, thoughts, and functions that make up a human being. Because the mind controls the body, illness truly begins in the mind.

◁ PLATO, *c.*400 BC
Western philosophy springs from Plato's definition of the Ideal as Love that is forever beautiful, good, and true.

▷ ARISTOTLE, *c.*300 BC
Through his investigation of all physical substances, this student of Plato concluded that the soul of every living thing is the breath of God.

◁ LAO-TZU, *c.*550 BC
The Chinese philosophy of the Tao has its roots in the teachings of this sage, who saw human life as a flow of events and activity that follows the natural order of the universe.

THE IMPETUS for the discipline we call *medical science* began in an era distinguished by masters of wisdom, including the Greek philosopher, Plato. Continuously searching to explain the universe, to connect what is eternal and unchanging with what is transient and insubstantial, these masters identified the ideals of beauty, truth, and goodness, and ascribed them to the mind of God. They gave expression to the laws of astronomy, physics, and mathematics, and viewed them as the speech of God. They regarded the human mind as infusing the body to create an indivisible unity of body, mind, and spirit. Perfect balance of these three entities ensures *wellness*; but if any one of them is out of balance, *dis-ease* and *illness* ensue.

DISINTEGRATION & SEPARATION

When science divorced religion in the seventeenth and eighteenth centuries, the poetic certainty and intuitive splendor of Plato and the great sages dimmed. Discussion of Platonic ideals resounded no more in academies of learning, and physicians lost sight of their main concern – to assist nature in accomplishing its own healing work.

HEALING THROUGH NATURE

Plant therapy has supported the repair and regeneration of the human form for hundreds of years. This picture shows a typical sixteenth-century pharmacy. Oil-preserved products and water-based extracts in glazed vessels appear behind and below dried herbs suspended in muslin bags. While a scribe records new recipes, an assistant is busy with mortar and pestle, and the chief apothecary attends to the needs of a young female customer.

Since that time, science without spirituality has developed into the technology that the western world recognizes as medicine today. In the widespread use of manufactured drugs, disease is conquered at a cellular level, while natural and kinder forms of healing, which are able to overcome disease through balancing the human ensemble, are often viewed skeptically and ridiculed as worthless.

No other concept has more profoundly shaped modern medicine than the myth advanced by individuals who affirm the dubious wisdom of science without spirituality. Surely it is the myth of a divided body, mind, and spirit that has encouraged a world without balance, where I-L-L is equivalent to I *Lack Love*.

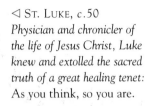

▷ THE BUDDHA, *c.*500 BC
Called The Buddha, the Indian teacher Gautama Siddhartha proclaimed that love and kindness alone dissolve animosity.

◁ ST. LUKE, *c.*50
Physician and chronicler of the life of Jesus Christ, Luke knew and extolled the sacred truth of a great healing tenet: As you think, so you are.

HEALING THE GREAT DIVIDE

What is before us now is an urgent need to discover the true path that will lead us back to health. Technology, unclasped from the merciful hand of spirituality, is taking a toll on our world that is increasingly destructive to humanity and the environment. Yet scientific evidence demonstrates that both *mental attitude* and *spiritual outlook* are determining factors for good health. Once more we are assured that science *with* spirituality knows no limitations.

▷ MAIMONIDES, 1150
For this Jewish physician, the Ideal consisted in the moral law of the Talmud and spiritual contentment through healthy living.

HEALTH CARE SYSTEMS – TIME FOR CHANGE

Long ago, our health was rooted in the Healing Force. This natural mechanism was supported by treatments that sought to restore health by balancing our energy.

Modern western medicine has changed our approach to healing. Body, mind, and spirit are treated not as a unity that strives for balance, but as separate entities.

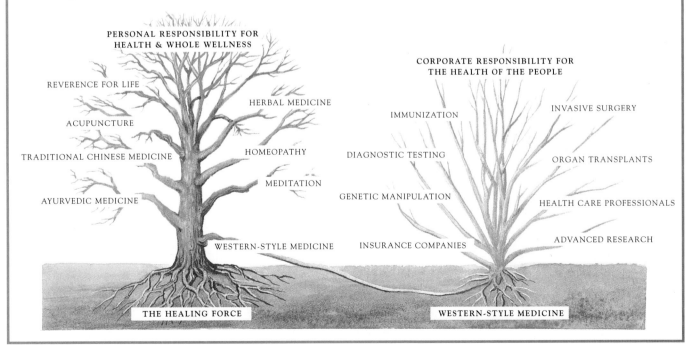

PERSONAL RESPONSIBILITY FOR
HEALTH & WHOLE WELLNESS

REVERENCE FOR LIFE

HERBAL MEDICINE

ACUPUNCTURE

TRADITIONAL CHINESE MEDICINE

HOMEOPATHY

MEDITATION

AYURVEDIC MEDICINE

WESTERN-STYLE MEDICINE

CORPORATE RESPONSIBILITY FOR
THE HEALTH OF THE PEOPLE

IMMUNIZATION

INVASIVE SURGERY

DIAGNOSTIC TESTING

ORGAN TRANSPLANTS

GENETIC MANIPULATION

HEALTH CARE PROFESSIONALS

INSURANCE COMPANIES

ADVANCED RESEARCH

THE HEALING FORCE

WESTERN-STYLE MEDICINE

ENERGY OUT OF BALANCE

Our bodies are more than just flesh and bones. They are systems of living, breathing, vital energy. Our energy connects us to the past and future, to the world in which we live, to each other, and to the great sea of life. Our existence is rooted in one common ground – the eternal source of energy that breathes life into each and every one of us. Whatever we touch touches others. But this truth has become concealed behind layers of misinformation and disharmony.

△ REACTION TO STRESS
It is not people and events that create your stress. Stress is created only by your own reaction and response to people and events. Therefore, stress begins in your mind.

△ DEPENDENCE ON MEDICATION
Over-the-counter and prescription medicines treat symptoms, but frequently interfere with your natural function and energy balance.

A SIGNIFICANT PART of the human energy system is its inborn meaning and purpose – its sense of balance. The presence of harmony and balance in our physical, mental, and spiritual energy results in perfect health and whole wellness. We can choose either to assist nature in accomplishing its healing work – to support our bodies with the nourishment we put into them, and by the loving nurture of our minds and spirits – or we can choose a descent into illness and disease by subjecting ourselves to the effects of stress.

Today, stress is affecting every man, woman, and child, ruining health, happiness, and life. Stress causes our energy to become out of balance and is the major cause of illness. Eating junk food; being addicted to harmful substances; getting little or no exercise; lacking a sense of purpose; and locking ourselves into loneliness, anger, and despair – all these are stressors, leading to imbalance.

Efforts to restore health and happiness should logically be efforts to restore balance to the human energy system. Yet treatment plans and procedures frequently fail to dislodge the deeper roots of illness.

Physical stressors *include eating processed foods more often than not; rarely eating fresh fruits and vegetables; getting very little or no exercise; taking over-the-counter medications for common problems such as indigestion and colds.*

Mental stressors *include being unable to cope positively with change; being worried, angry, and resentful; not forgiving; feeling lonely, despondent, and not connected to the universe.*

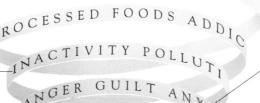

PROCESSED FOODS ADDIC
INACTIVITY POLLUTI
ANGER GUILT ANXI
LONELINESS
LACK OF LOVE
UNETHICAL
BEHAVI
FEAR

ILLEGAL DRUGS

COFFEE   TEA

HABITS & ADDICTIONS
Harmful substances hinder the free flow of energy in your body.

Spiritual stressors *include living in the past; having no belief in a sacred presence; believing that the universe is unfriendly; having no personal code of honor or purpose in life; lacking self-esteem; being self-centered; feeling unloved.*

DESCENT INTO ILLNESS

The human ensemble is a self-regulating mechanism that functions according to how it is treated. Pollution and other physical stressors are known to be harmful to health, but the inability to process stress is equally so, because stress is transmuted into imbalance and disease.

Hailed as marvels of research and medical technology, medications and surgery may provide nothing more than temporary relief from symptoms of disease. Our minds have become programmed into an expectation of illness. Our intuitive knowledge of wellness is cast into veiled shadows of illusion – media messages that would lead us to believe that we have no choice but to accept illness and disease.

THE HEALING FORCE – AWAKENING THE SPIRIT

Such messages teach us that it is easier to medicate illness than to change the behaviors that may have caused the illness in the first place – and quicker, also. Particularly for individuals approaching old age, illness and ill health are presented as inevitable. The best we can do for our bodies, we are told, is to medicate them while we wait for the next wave of disease – be it heart attack, stroke, breast cancer, AIDS, osteoporosis, and more – and if disease does not get us, natural decline and the anticipation of illness surely will.

Fortunately, our dreams and visions of the future need not center on fear and the anticipation of disease. Every illness is anchored in an imbalance of energy – therefore, our health is determined by personal responsibility, self-value, and reverence for life. The real choice we have is *not* to become dependent on doctors, hospitals, surgical procedures, and medications, but to learn how to fan the flames of our Healing Force, awakening its spirit and setting its sail on a calm sea of balanced energy.

We are what we think.
All that we are arises
with our thoughts.
With our thoughts
we make the world.

GAUTAMA SIDDHARTHA
(THE BUDDHA)

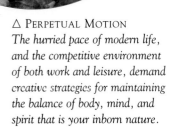

△ PERPETUAL MOTION
The hurried pace of modern life, and the competitive environment of both work and leisure, demand creative strategies for maintaining the balance of body, mind, and spirit that is your inborn nature.

◁ RESTORATIVE VISION
Taking moments during the day to recreate a magical experience in your mind, or simply to dwell on pleasant thoughts, can restore your faith in your ability to cope with the stresses of everyday life.

THE HEALING TESTAMENT

Except for western medical science, almost all traditions of medicine are based on the concept of life-energy. All share a fundamental understanding of energy as the vital force that flows through every living thing in the universe. Indian medicine calls this vital force prana. *Chinese medicine calls it ch'i. These traditions treat illness and disease in ways that stimulate the Healing Force, realign energy, and restore balance.*

HIPPOCRATES, c.400 BC
Generally held to be the father of medicine, Hippocrates believed that the four elements of earth, air, water, and fire are mirrored in the human body by the humors – black bile, yellow bile, phlegm, and blood. When the humors are out of balance, illness results.

PLANTS FOR GOOD HEALTH
Once, oils infused with plant essences filled the shelves of the pharmacy. The myrtle oil in this jar was said to strengthen the nerves and brain as well as weak limbs and joints.

IN TUNE with the wisdom of the East, physicians in the modern western world recognize the existence of a physical force within the body that keeps it at peace with itself – that maintains its inborn sense of balance. Perceptive individuals recognize also that the resources of our minds and spirits are a crucial part of the total strategy for treating illness and disease. Thus is born a concept for the new millennium, where the best of western science is integrated with the awareness of the East. This concept is the healing testament that offers us whole wellness and health.

SHIFTING ILLNESS TO WELLNESS

Observing the disintegration of our world, it comes as little surprise that we should wonder (in the words of our modern fable at right): *What on earth is going on upstream?* Vast intelligence is not required to understand that treating the appearance of disease, rather than dislodging its root cause, is an unlikely prescription for health.

It is impossible to overestimate the magnitude behind the shift of vision that will open the door to wellness. While an expectation of illness encumbers us with the self-fulfilling prophecy of decline, punctuated with inevitable waves of disease, anticipating the best possible health arouses the spirit of our Healing Force. This is the source of balance that is forever capable of being illumined.

WHOLE WELLNESS & BEYOND

The notion that we can control our health destiny far beyond what we were taught to believe possible has become the immutable and eternal ideal for our time. Once again, we can identify and strive towards what is forever beautiful, good, and true – by taking the healing testament into our lives. Here is a strategy of simple baby steps for change that restores energy balance, promotes wellness, and places us in a position of self-determination and power.

ASCENT INTO WELLNESS & HEALTH

New wisdom about healthful living is based on a commonsense approach that is often rejected in favor of transitory trends. Yet such wisdom strikes an ancient chord that is attuned to the instrument of wellness, inspiring the realization that health is chiefly determined by personal responsibility, self-value, and reverence for life.

Spiritual abettors include staying in the here and now; identifying the Ideal and striving towards it; recognizing a sacred presence in every living thing; knowing that Goodness and Love are the most powerful healers of all.

Mental abettors include being willing to forgive; seeing the joy in life; fulfilling your potential; engaging in lifelong learning; feeling connected to the universe; having a sense of accomplishment; treating people with compassion.

LOVE
SERVICE
CODE OF HO
PRAYER RESPE
MEDITATION &
LIFELONG LEARNING
REGULAR EXERCISE
FRESH FOODS LAUGHTER

HERBAL MEDICINE
Treatments based on plants stimulate the inner balance that lies at the heart of wellness.

Physical abettors include getting sufficient rest; avoiding addictive substances such as alcohol and caffeine; getting regular exercise; eating energy-filled food; meditating daily; remembering moderation in all things.

REGULAR MODERATE EXERCISE
The ascent to wellness is incomplete without regular and enjoyable activity. Yoga is ideal, creating a supple body, a focused mind, and a spirit that feels at peace with the world.

FRESH FOODS FROM THE SOIL
Eating live food – food that grows in the soil and is fresh and filled with the life-energy of the sun – contributes greatly to high levels of wellness. Fresh fruits and vegetables are ideal. They are the source of optimal energy and the building blocks of your healthful eating plan.

WHAT ON EARTH IS GOING ON UPSTREAM?

The idyllic town of Downstream is located where a sparkling stream enters a river. A small community raises its families, makes a decent living in the button factory, and exists in quiet harmony together. One day, to the amazement of all, a few weakened and ill people are found floating in the stream. Not from Downstream (where wellness prevails), but requiring help, they are rescued, and nurtured back to good health by the kindly townspeople.

As ever more similarly sick people are found floating in the stream, a need arises for legions of medical technicians, general practitioners, and surgeons, and a huge array of support services that are housed in skyscrapers – land, once plentiful, has become a scarce commodity. Now, the peaceful community of Downstream is extremely busy and so gainfully employed that no one has the time, or the insight, to wonder: *What on earth is going on upstream?*

The first thing we have to say respecting what are called *new views* here in New England, at the present time, Is that they are not new, but the very oldest of thoughts, Cast into the mold of these new times.

RALPH WALDO EMERSON, 1842

WHOLE WELLNESS – THE NEW IDEAL

Wise physicians already understand that the spiritual, physiological, and psychological resources of their patients are – along with the best that modern medicine has to offer – an important part of any total treatment strategy. Whole wellness embraces this understanding in the concept of a dynamic partnership between physician and patient, and in so doing affords individuals the maximum expression for their inner healing potential.

From everlasting I was firmly set, from the beginning: the deep was not, when I was born … there were no springs to gush water. Before the mountains were settled, before the hills, I came to birth.

THE BIBLE

FROM conception to death, the life cycle of every human being is akin to a spiritual pilgrimage. We are like animated stardust, children of the universe, awaiting the moment of our return home. Yet, while traveling back to our source, we are much greater than a collection of skin, muscle, tissue, and bone. Both physically and mentally, we are self-repairing energy systems, comprising an inner compass, ever-replicating spirals of DNA, and a biological clock.

A CONSCIOUS SHIFT TO EMPOWER CHANGE

Such concepts are not easy to approach in a medical climate that is so greatly focused on the metabolic and infectious causes of disease. What is required is a shift in consciousness from illness to wellness. Whole Wellness provides the ideal model for such a shift, enabling far greater control of our own health destiny than was ever thought possible. It extends way beyond prescriptions and treatment plans into empowerment and change, and soars into the realms of health nurtured by personal responsibility, self-value, and reverence for life.

THE FOUR ASPECTS OF HEALTH & WHOLE WELLNESS

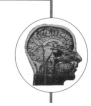

THE BIOLOGICAL CLOCK
Self-replicating DNA transmits the genetic information for every individual from generation to generation – see p.17.

MIND–BODY CONNECTIONS
In the intimate ensemble of mind and body, what is on your mind and in your heart can make you sick or keep you well – see p.18.

ENERGY SYSTEMS
Much more than the sum of its various parts, the human body is a collection of myriad cells that vibrate with energy – see p.19.

THE INNER COMPASS
The rightful equilibrium of body, mind, and spirit is maintained by an inner compass set towards remembered wellness – see p.20.

THE BIOLOGICAL CLOCK

Each of your physical and mental characteristics is carried in your genes, which in addition provide for an inborn biological clock that signals adolescence, adulthood, and old age. While the principal purpose of genes is to enable both the preservation and the protection of our species, disease-carrying genes are still a part of every individual. Fortunately for us, these genes, which contain templates of most of the diseases of our ancestors, do not determine our destiny. Instead, they must answer to our inner compass, which remembers wellness and keeps the templates safely stored away.

strong, wiry physique

diabetes mellitus

curly dark hair

heart disease

visual creativity

TEMPLATES OF DISEASE

The templates of the diseases that are carried in our genes – diseases such as asthma, arthritis, diabetes, colitis, and obesity – are usually locked in guarded vaults within our cells, for all time. Few templates are meant ever to appear, and those that are must wait for correct signals from our body's biological clock. Thus, certain types of disease tend naturally to appear at certain stages of life (see below). But when our energy is out of balance, the templates of disease emerge in an untimely fashion, prematurely. Processed foods, inactivity, anxiety, fear, addictions, and environmental pollution all help to damage our cellular vaults, and to create imbalance. Most diseases we now experience are no more than the result of templates of diseases that are appearing before due time.

△ COMPUTER MODEL OF DNA
DNA is the substance that contains the genetic coding for each species of living thing. Encoded in our own human DNA is a vast quantity of information, including the templates of disease, that we have been inheriting since our families began – it is said, over 60 million years ago.

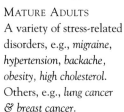

INFANTS	CHILDREN	YOUNG ADULTS	MATURE ADULTS	OLDER ADULTS
Metabolic diseases, e.g., *cystic fibrosis.* Congenital malformations, e.g., *heart disease, cleft lip & cleft palate, hip dysplasia.*	Immune system diseases, e.g., *asthma, eczema.* Behavioral diseases, e.g., *attention deficit disorder.* Others, e.g., *leukemia, Type I diabetes, allergy.*	Genitourinary diseases, e.g., *cervical cancer.* Gastrointestinal diseases, e.g., *colitis, enteritis, ulcers.* Neuropsychiatric diseases, e.g., *schizophrenia.*	A variety of stress-related disorders, e.g., *migraine, hypertension, backache, obesity, high cholesterol.* Others, e.g., *lung cancer & breast cancer.*	Blood vessel diseases, e.g., *heart attack, stroke.* Bone & joint disorders, e.g., *osteoporosis, arthritis.* Neoplastic diseases, e.g., *prostate & uterine cancers.*

17

MIND–BODY CONNECTIONS

BELIEF BECOMES SUBSTANCE
A dragon dance celebrates the Chinese New Year, a day on which the gates to heaven are believed to swing open. In the week before, when entry is less easily attained, death rates plummet, rising dramatically the week after.

PSYCHONEUROIMMUNOLOGY is the name of the science that documents the relationship between mind and body – and the ways in which thoughts, feelings, and emotions influence not only health but also the appearance and course of disease. Calling this science "mind–body connections" helps to make the findings of its research more comprehensible, presenting us with information that we can wisely use to help restore the balance of our energy.

That the mind has the ability to be either slayer or healer is one of the most important findings. What is on your mind, and in your heart, *can* make you sick or keep you well. Toxic emotions, such as unresolved conflict and fear, anger, worry, loneliness, and despair, send your body a "die" message – while forgiveness, love, kindness, and hope become transformed into powerful natural medicines that invite peace of mind and send messages of healing and life.

A NETWORK OF COMMUNICATION

The intricate network of communication within your body takes every impulse of your mind and translates it into a chemical reaction that affects the balance of your energy. Healing chemicals are released whenever you do things that make you feel good about yourself. Actions, attitudes, and expectations do have physical consequences. Thus, accepting personal responsibility for your own health – recognizing the power you have to determine your health destiny through your mind – is the first step on the path towards optimal wellness.

INSTINCT & EXPECTATION – CONNECTING MIND WITH BODY

The two simple experiments that are described here demonstrate the power of instinct and expectation in determining our physical health. While instinct is an intuitive tool for survival, expectation is wholly within our control. Though done with mice, these experiments have results that are equally relevant to our discussion of the connections between human minds and bodies.

In experiment one, small boxes of candy-coated breakfast cereal were put in cages with mice. The mice ate the cardboard cereal boxes but consistently left the cereal alone. *Survival instinct* told them that the cardboard was more nourishing than the cereal.

In experiment two, the mice were repeatedly fed poison mixed with a harmless substance that had a very distinctive taste. Again and again they became sick, but were nursed back to health. Finally, they were fed only the substance without the poison, and again became sick. *Expectation* told them that the distinctive-tasting substance alone was harmful to them.

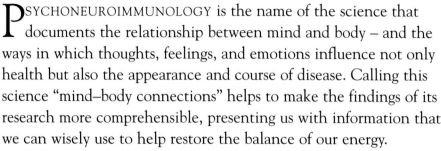

ENERGY SYSTEMS

THE nineteenth-century French novelist, Marcel Proust, wrote: *The real voyage of discovery consists not in seeking new landscapes, but in having new eyes.* When we consider the human body as more than the sum of its various parts, and recognize it as a collection of cells vibrating with energy, we can see our selves through new eyes. Then, rather than being constrained by *information*, we can expand our *wisdom* and begin regarding our bodies in a new light.

DISCORD & DISHARMONY

Consider this musical analogy. Violins playing a symphony produce sound that is simply energy. When their strings vibrate in harmony with each other, the notes are resonant and the melody is clear. An orchestra creates harmony when every instrument plays in tune. Its sound energy, which we hear as tuneful music, is in balance. But if the violins are out of tune, the sound energy of the entire orchestra becomes out of balance, so that we hear discord and disharmony.

In the body, discord occurs when the energy of its cells is out of balance. Western medicine uses labels of diseases such as *asthma* or *diabetes* or *cancer* for this discord. Thus we perceive that illness and disease are simply discord in our bodies – energy out of balance.

TUNEFUL HARMONY & ACCORD

As with violins playing in tune, when the cells of an organ vibrate in harmony with each other, that organ performs its functions well. It is in balance, able to experience wellness. Observe a colorful object. In the moment of observation, myriad vibrations occur in the cells of your eyes, and send messages to the part of your brain that controls vision.

It is estimated that in this moment, each eye cell produces countless vibrations, more than all the waves that have ever touched the shores of all the world's great oceans since the beginning of recorded history.

Again, as with the orchestra, when each organ and system of our bodies is in balance, it is as if every instrument is playing in tune. Then the energy systems that are our bodies sing in harmony, and we experience the gift of life as a state of vibrant, radiant wellness.

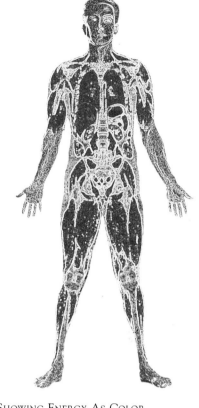

SHOWING ENERGY AS COLOR
The visual expression of new ideas is often helpful in understanding them. Instead of viewing internal anatomy as countless cells vibrating together, this computer image uses colors to indicate the major muscles, organs, and bone structure of a male body.

HOLDING LIFE IN BALANCE
In this protective amulet, eight trigrams (the key to knowledge) encircle the symbols of yin and yang, which represent the opposing yet complementary principles of the universe. In the human ensemble, the Healing Force holds these principles in balance, and nurtures the body's harmony through waves of energy that expand and contract. Thus we are assured a lifetime of wellness while we travel joyfully back to our source.

THE INNER COMPASS

WHEEL OF LIFE
This circle of images depicts each stage of the eternal dance of life. Following the path of harmony and balance by our inner compass ensures a smooth journey back to our source.

HUMAN beings are not programmed to self destruct. Rather, our genes are intended to enable the preservation, protection, and survival of our species. This intention exists, deep within the heart of every individual, as Remembered Wellness: the infinite, eternal wisdom of the spirit that fuses body and mind together in healthful and dynamic equilibrium – and is maintained by our inner compass that is pulled always towards wellness. Remembered Wellness exists even behind veils of illness and disease, continuously attempting to create harmony, restore balance, and maintain life.

BREAKTHROUGH TO WELLNESS

This truth remains, however out of balance (however ill) the body may be. Thus, it is always possible to experience a breakthrough to wellness. Overnight cures, spontaneous remissions – such "miracles of healing" occur daily. Yet the words of Saint Augustine remind us that *miracles never contradict nature; miracles only contradict what we know about nature*. It is, after all, not so difficult to revive our spirit of Remembered Wellness, to embark on our own personal voyage to wellness with its landfalls of nutrition, exercise, and de-addiction, its spiritual buoys of meditation, self-esteem, forgiveness, and love.

The cerebellum is a rounded structure that is located behind the brain stem (see below right). It is primarily concerned with maintaining posture and sense of balance, and coordinating body movements.

CENTERS OF TRUE BALANCE

In this colored nuclear magnetic resonance scan of a section through a normal brain, its main structures – the cerebellum, the cerebrum, and the brain stem – are clearly visible. Although sophisticated technology and methods of evaluating brain function have increased our knowledge of its structure, the precise way in which it works, and how mind–body connections are made, continues to elude modern science. Trust in intuitive centers of balance such as Remembered Wellness may prove worthy of more serious study.

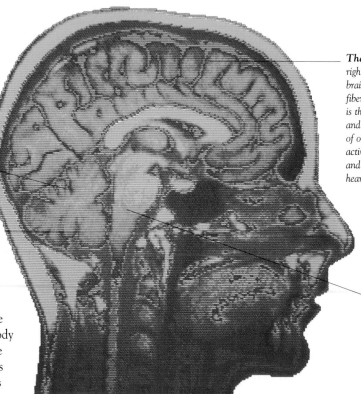

The cerebrum consists of the right and left hemispheres of the brain joined by a band of white fibers, the corpus callosum. It is the largest part of the brain, and the control center for most of our conscious and intelligent activities – including emotion and feeling as well as behavior, hearing, speech, and vision.

The brain stem, forming the lowest part of the brain, links the cerebrum and cerebellum with the spinal cord, which is protected within the spinal column. It is responsible for the control of vital functions such as breathing, digestion, and blood circulation.

RESPONSIBLE COMPLEMENTARY MEDICINE

The most effective health care seeks to strengthen and balance the energies of body, mind, and spirit so that our inner compass points always towards wellness. Western scientific medicine enhances and prolongs life by relieving specific symptoms of illness and removing diseased parts of the body. Many older traditions of healing combine an understanding of the human ensemble as a threefold unity with gentler methods of treatment that restore and maintain health by stimulating the spirit of Remembered Wellness. These traditions can be called *Responsible Complementary Medicine*.

⁓ Ayurveda is the ancient healing science of India. It embraces a code of healthful living and a natural treatment system in which purity of mind is necessary for encouraging physical health through the strength and flow of *prana* – the vital life force. Ayurveda aims to eliminate the root cause of disease by promoting moderation and balance between human beings and their environment. All aspects of living are involved in inspiring prana to create harmony within the human ensemble. Thus, ethics, emotions, and devotion assume equal importance with climate, good nutrition, and exercise.

⁓ Homeopathy treats disease by administering extremely small quantities of remedies from animal, vegetable, and mineral sources. These remedies bolster natural healing forces that have the power to neutralize the destructive forces of disease. Diagnosis is made by careful consideration of feelings, reactions, and personality type, as well as physical symptoms, in order to construct a complete portrait of the patient. Remedies are formulated in different concentrations but – theoretically – all would produce the very symptoms they are prescribed to relieve, if used in much larger quantities.

⁓ Traditional Chinese Medicine regards good health as the result of a perfectly balanced interplay between opposing yet complementary forces. All life contains such forces, which are enshrined in the principles of *yin* and *yang*. The essential energy of life – its vital force, *ch'i* – is believed to peak when yin and yang are in harmony not only within the patient's body, but in the patient's life as a whole. The effectiveness of acupuncture and herbal medicine, which lie at the heart of Traditional Chinese Medicine, is based on their ability to balance yin with yang and encourage the steady flow of ch'i.

▷ HERBAL TINCTURE
Walnut can be useful during times of change, when relinquishing old habits and ideas is difficult.

◁ ACUPUNCTURE NEEDLES
Inserting these slender needles along known lines of energy, called meridians, *removes impediments to the free flow of the vital life force, ch'i.*

▷ SIX DISTINCT TASTES
In Ayurveda, one or more of six tastes – sweet, sour, bitter, pungent, astringent, salty – is used to describe the healing properties of different herbs and fruits.

◁ MEDITATION
Prana, the life force in Ayurvedic medicine, *is represented here in the symbol, OM. Holding an image or symbol in the mind can be a help during meditation.*

▷ PLANT ESSENCES
Juniper has been associated with cleansing for more than 5,000 years and is highly regarded for its antiseptic properties.

◁ REMEDIES FROM NATURE
Western-style medications are often concoctions of chemicals imitating active ingredients that were once found in the natural formulas of herbal remedies.

WELLNESS EN

ERGY PROFILE

EVALUATING YOUR WELLNESS

Wellness is the dance of life that celebrates infinite & eternal harmony. It is the dynamic activity of caring for your body as the home for your soul; the enriching quality of striving to fulfill your highest potential; and the elevating state of filling your life with love. To achieve wellness is to attain the point of balance where the energies of body, mind, and spirit are so finely attuned to each other that distinctions between them fade away.

IN THIS section of the book, you are encouraged to evaluate your wellness levels and energy balance by completing a series of specially designed questionnaires.

There are fifteen questionnaires, divided into three sets of five each (see box below, *Wellness Energy – Keeping Life in a State of Balance*). They help you hold up a mirror to yourself to reflect upon your levels of personal responsibility, self-value, and reverence for life. This analysis is your essential preparation for the Wellness Action Plan.

As well as providing you with a unique tool for self-assessment, the questionnaires are also designed to stimulate learning, commitment, and the will to change and develop. They are not intended either to be judgmental or to induce feelings of despondency, inadequacy, or guilt. Endeavor, therefore, to respond to the questionnaires with gentleness and compassion for yourself, even if your image appears imperfect.

HEALING IS A PROCESS

The purpose of understanding your current state and level of wellness is to inspire change and to promote improvement on all levels. No one is perfect: there is always room for improvement *no matter how small it may be*. Your objective is to begin the empowering process of bringing your physical, mental, and spiritual energy into greater balance so that the ultimate source of your strength emerges – your Healing Force.

Yet there is no *quick fix*. Healing is, after all, a process, not an event. This process begins with assisting nature in her healing work instead of allowing yourself to succumb to the effects of stress. Your mind can be healer or slayer. What is on your mind and in your heart thus has a profound effect on your health.

Ascending the *Pyramid of Human Aspiration* is the Wellness Action Plan (pages 50 to 153) that guides you to take control of your health destiny. Its easy steps add up to the sustained effort that will improve and enhance your energy balance.

WELLNESS ENERGY – KEEPING LIFE IN A STATE OF BALANCE

ASSESSING YOUR BODY'S WELLNESS
Nutrition, Exercise, Hygiene & Safety, De-medication, and De-addiction are the five factors that determine the balance of your physical energy – see pp.26–31.

ASSESSING YOUR MIND'S WELLNESS
Happiness, Kindness & Empathy, Learning, Self-esteem, and Ethics are the five factors that determine the balance of your mental energy – see pp.32–37.

ASSESSING YOUR SPIRIT'S WELLNESS
Harmlessness, Awareness, Lovingness, Faith & Devotion, and Transcendence & Joy are the five factors that determine the balance of your spiritual energy – see pp.38–43.

MAKING YOUR ASSESSMENT

Now you are ready to approach the task of self-assessment. Before you answer the questionnaires, make at least one photocopy of each one so that you can re-evaluate your state of wellness one month from now. Reserve at least one uninterrupted hour of time. Then, still your mind with this brief exercise.

Find a comfortable, quiet place where you will not be disturbed. *Close your eyes and take seven long, deep, even breaths. As you exhale, consciously relax each muscle in your body. Be aware of how much stress is harbored in your muscles. Imagine a warm, golden light that radiates from your heart to every part of your body. Be aware that the warmth and power of this golden light can dissolve stress throughout your entire being.*

Now, feeling calm and relaxed, go on to the questionnaires. Each consists of 24–30 statements. Read each statement carefully and check it *only if it applies to you.* Try not to overanalyze any statement – simply trust in your intuition, make a swift decision, and move on to the next statement. Check a statement that seems only partially applicable *if it is more applicable than not.*

NAMING THE SACRED

Finally, take a momentary pause to reflect on the following wisdom.

Sensing a sacred presence in life has been the inspiration for many wonders created by human hands. This inspiration is neither limited to particular belief systems – nor is it the preserve of specific religions.

Sacredness, while beyond words, is nevertheless defined in the word, God. But let us conceptualize God simply as love, the inner unity, and divine essence and source of life.

A tree as great as a man's embrace springs from a small shoot. A terrace nine stories high begins with a pile of earth. A journey of a thousand miles starts with the first step.

LAO-TZU

ASSESSING YOUR BODY'S WELLNESS

In this era of stress, your health is primarily determined by personal responsibility, self-value, and reverence for life. Even the smallest efforts towards better self-care can encourage the flow of your healing energy that restores balance. Thus, the journey towards wellness is as important as the goal. Embracing wellness activities inspires you to feel good about yourself, which in turn stimulates the spirit of remembered wellness.

It is the best of humanity that goes out to walk. In happy hours, all affairs may be postponed For walking.

RALPH WALDO EMERSON

WELLNESS is much more than the absence of disease. This is why the *Energy Balance Scales* are not based on symptoms of illness.

Ultimately, your health depends more on what you are willing to do for yourself rather than what others are willing to do for you. To restore your energy balance, you need first to assess what is causing imbalance in your physical energy. The main factors are improper nutrition, lack of exercise, and foreign chemicals such as sugar, alcohol, and tobacco.

Your physical energy balance scale reflects how well you take care of your body. The information gained by completing the questionnaires is critical to your health, but it does not *automatically* generate positive action for healthful change.

The most reliable way to ensure change is to awaken your reverence for life – all life, *including your own.* This paradigm shift from illness to wellness occurs as you rise through the seven steps of the Pyramid and is completed as you reach the goal.

WORKING METHOD

Read each statement and check it *only* if it applies to you. If the statement appears only partially applicable, check it if it is *more applicable than not.* Identify the score for each of your checked statements, calculate your total score, and write it in the box. **Important Note** *Make sure to cover up the scorecard while you work through each questionnaire.*

NUTRITION QUESTIONNAIRE

Nutrition is the dynamic activity of eating wholesome foods that nourish body, mind, and spirit. A nurturing diet emphasizes foods that replenish the body with vital energy instead of draining energy in the process of digestion.

1. I will go out of my way to buy the freshest produce.
2. I am a "meat and potatoes" kind of person.
3. I eat lots of fresh fruit and vegetables every day.
4. My usual meal is something I've opened with a can opener, or unfrozen, or microwaved.
5. I regularly eat fried or greasy foods.
6. I drink plenty of water each day.
7. I regularly eat so much food that I feel uncomfortable.
8. Complex carbohydrates (potatoes, pasta, rice, beans, and whole grain bread) and fresh fruits and vegetables make up the greater part of my diet.
9. I rarely eat junk food.
10. I often suffer with gas, constipation, or diarrhea.
11. I prefer fresh foods to processed.
12. I don't use much butter or gravy, and use other heavy sauces sparingly.
13. I am just about the right weight.
14. I'd like to be a vegetarian.
15. I drink lots of milk and regularly consume other dairy products.

16. I often have indigestion, heartburn, or gallbladder or other intestinal problems.
17. Cooking a nutritious, healthy meal can be great fun.
18. I am very obese (more than 50 pounds overweight).
19. I am moderately obese (between 25 and 50 pounds overweight).
20. Fresh-squeezed fruit juice is best.
21. I don't have time to make healthy meals.
22. Most of the time I skip breakfast, or just eat doughnuts, pastries, or eggs.
23. I'll take the time to prepare a healthy meal just for me.
24. I eat fresh vegetables as a snack.
25. I am a vegetarian.
26. I don't need meat to be strong and healthy.
27. I gobble my food.
28. My diet is mostly vegetarian (it includes chicken and fish, but no red meat).
29. I love salads.
30. I don't eat red meat.

SCORECARD

1. +3	4. −2	7. −3	10. −2	13. +3	16. −2	19. −2	22. −2	25. +3	28. +3
2. −1	5. −2	8. +3	11. +2	14. +1	17. +2	20. +2	23. +2	26. +2	29. +3
3. +3	6. +1	9. +2	12. +1	15. −2	18. −3	21. −2	24. +2	27. −2	30. +3

TOTAL

EXERCISE QUESTIONNAIRE

Exercise is the dynamic activity of developing balanced energy that strengthens your body and calms your mind. Exercise revitalizes your body's storehouse of energy, stimulates your Healing Force, and inspires inner confidence and firm resolve.

1. I consider myself in very good shape for my age.
2. I don't think I could ever get myself in better shape.
3. I engage in some form of vigorous physical activity, which makes me sweaty or breathe faster, for 20 minutes at least three times a week.
4. If I walk up a flight of stairs, I am out of breath at the top.
5. I dislike exercise and avoid it whenever I can.
6. I often climb stairs instead of taking elevators.
7. I am not a "couch potato."
8. I love walking and walk regularly.
9. I belong to a health club and use it regularly.
10. I regularly go to an exercise class.
11. I'm too old to start exercising.
12. I consider myself a very active person.
13. I have had hypertension, a heart attack, or a stroke, **and** I still do not regularly engage in any form of physical exercise.
14. Even the idea of yoga seems ridiculous to me.

15. I've tried exercise, but I can never stick with it.
16. Exercise or playing sports has always been a part of my life.
17. I feel out of sorts if I don't get my exercise.
18. When I've tried exercising, I usually overdo, and then I hurt myself.
19. I don't have time to exercise.
20. Many members of my family, and many of my friends, enjoy exercise.
21. Where I live, you can't get out to exercise.
22. I don't have enough energy to exercise.
23. I enjoy yoga.
24. Exercise doesn't do you any good.
25. My work requires a good deal of physical exertion.
26. Exercise is fun for me.
27. I believe that exercise is crucial for good health.
28. I regularly do stretching and flexing exercises.
29. My body is not very flexible.
30. Exercise is very helpful to overcome stress, sadness, and depression.

SCORECARD

1. +3	4. −2	7. +2	10. +2	13. −3	16. +3	19. −2	22. −2	25. +2	28. +3
2. −3	5. −3	8. +3	11. −3	14. −1	17. +2	20. +2	23. +3	26. +2	29. −1
3. +3	6. +3	9. +2	12. +3	15. −1	18. −1	21. −1	24. −2	27. +3	30. +3

TOTAL

HYGIENE & SAFETY QUESTIONNAIRE

Personal hygiene and safety are the dynamic activities of caring for your body as the haven for your soul. Respecting and honoring your body protects and encourages your Healing Force in its work, so that your whole being radiates life-energy.

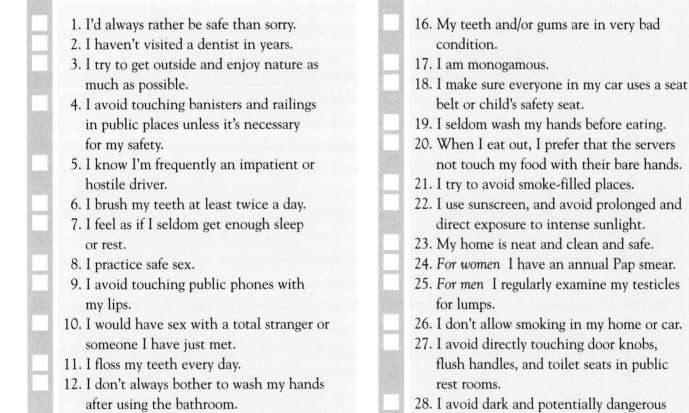

1. I'd always rather be safe than sorry.
2. I haven't visited a dentist in years.
3. I try to get outside and enjoy nature as much as possible.
4. I avoid touching banisters and railings in public places unless it's necessary for my safety.
5. I know I'm frequently an impatient or hostile driver.
6. I brush my teeth at least twice a day.
7. I feel as if I seldom get enough sleep or rest.
8. I practice safe sex.
9. I avoid touching public phones with my lips.
10. I would have sex with a total stranger or someone I have just met.
11. I floss my teeth every day.
12. I don't always bother to wash my hands after using the bathroom.
13. *For women* I do a breast self-examination once a month.
14. I lock my doors and secure my home at night.
15. I keep my body very clean.
16. My teeth and/or gums are in very bad condition.
17. I am monogamous.
18. I make sure everyone in my car uses a seat belt or child's safety seat.
19. I seldom wash my hands before eating.
20. When I eat out, I prefer that the servers not touch my food with their bare hands.
21. I try to avoid smoke-filled places.
22. I use sunscreen, and avoid prolonged and direct exposure to intense sunlight.
23. My home is neat and clean and safe.
24. *For women* I have an annual Pap smear.
25. *For men* I regularly examine my testicles for lumps.
26. I don't allow smoking in my home or car.
27. I avoid directly touching door knobs, flush handles, and toilet seats in public rest rooms.
28. I avoid dark and potentially dangerous places.
29. On occasion, I'll drive while intoxicated.
30. I'm engaged in a healthy, loving, committed sexual relationship.

SCORECARD

1. +3	4. +2	7. −2	10. −3	13. +3	16. −2	19. −2	22. +3	25. +3	28. +3
2. −2	5. −3	8. +3	11. +2	14. +3	17. +3	20. +1	23. +2	26. +3	29. −3
3. +3	6. +2	9. +1	12. −2	15. +3	18. +3	21. +2	24. +3	27. +2	30. +3

TOTAL

DE-MEDICATION QUESTIONNAIRE

De-medication is the dynamic activity of freeing yourself from excess medications. It is a process of cleansing your body of unnecessary drugs that impede energy flow. De-medication begins with your awareness of nature's unlimited power to heal.

1. You can't tinker with the body's natural metabolism without expecting some difficulty or harm to occur.
2. Medications have always been a part of my life.
3. I look for natural alternatives to medications and drugs.
4. I avoid medication for minor problems whenever I can.
5. My parents generally avoided using medications and drugs.
6. I'd need a huge medicine cabinet to hold all my medicines and prescriptions.
7. I rarely need to visit my doctor.
8. I try to avoid indigestion by eating properly.
9. I'd rather fix the root cause of a problem than just medicate it.
10. I can't remember many days in my life without medicines.
11. If I'm not feeling well, I would insist that my doctor prescribe medication to help.
12. I believe that as you age, you need many more medications.
13. Rather than medicate a cold, I'd let it run its course.
14. I generally feel that there is a medicine for every ailment, illness, ache, or pain.
15. I don't take sleeping medications.

16. I believe that people are much too dependent upon their physicians.
17. I often take medicine for indigestion.
18. Children should have the least possible amount of medication.
19. Alternative treatments such as acupuncture and herbs are generally a waste of time.
20. I have frequent backaches and headaches, and medicate them with painkillers.
21. I take a tranquilizer when I'm stressed.
22. I'd be greatly disappointed if I came away from a doctor's office visit without a prescription in hand.
23. My health is primarily my responsibility.
24. I use lots of laxatives.
25. Overall, I think that people tend to use way too many medicines.
26. I don't mind eating food that I know will give me indigestion; I can always ease the discomfort with medication.
27. I believe that rest and sunshine can be as important as medicine and drugs.
28. Medication may cause as many problems as it helps.
29. I feel very well most of the time and have no need for medications.
30. I believe it's more important to add life to my years than years to my life.

SCORECARD

1. +3	4. +1	7. +3	10. −2	13. +2	16. +2	19. −2	22. −2	25. +2	28. +2
2. −1	5. +1	8. +3	11. −3	14. −2	17. −2	20. −2	23. +3	26. −3	29. +3
3. +3	6. −2	9. +3	12. −1	15. +1	18. +3	21. −2	24. −2	27. +2	30. +3

TOTAL

DE-ADDICTION QUESTIONNAIRE

De-addiction is the dynamic activity of releasing yourself from substances and habits that harm your body, mind, and spirit. De-addiction strengthens your self-value, reverence for life, and care for the soul, so that harmful habits melt away.

1. I am not a smoker.
2. I wish I could stop smoking but I'm hooked.
3. I do not use recreational drugs (marijuana, cocaine, uppers, downers, etc.).
4. I don't want to stop smoking because I enjoy it.
5. I don't smoke cigars or use a pipe.
6. I don't chew tobacco.
7. Alcohol is not an essential part of my life.
8. I regularly need alcohol to help me relax and unwind.
9. I have one or two alcoholic drinks just about every day.
10. I have more than two alcoholic drinks almost every day.
11. I love a drink at the end of a hard day.
12. Most of my friends don't drink or drink in moderation.
13. Most of my friends don't smoke.
14. Most of my friends don't use drugs.
15. I would never go to work drunk or stoned.
16. A drink or two at lunchtime doesn't do any harm.
17. I drink more than four sodas or diet sodas a week.
18. I drink less than four sodas or diet sodas a week.
19. I drink more than three cups of coffee or tea a day.
20. I think clearly without coffee or other stimulants.
21. I avoid drinking because I sometimes suspect I'm an alcoholic.
22. Most of my social activities revolve around drinking.
23. I'll have candy, ice cream, or other sweets most days of the week.
24. I regularly binge – to the point of not feeling well – on large amounts of candy, ice cream, or sweets.
25. I rarely eat salty snacks and don't add much salt to my food.
26. I'll drive after drinking too much.
27. I often use sleeping pills.
28. I have an addictive personality and often give in to it.
29. My personality changes after a couple of drinks.
30. I have no addictions or detrimental habits.

SCORECARD

1. +3	4. −3	7. +3	10. −3	13. +3	16. −2	19. −2	22. −2	25. +3	28. −3
2. −3	5. +2	8. −3	11. 0	14. +3	17. −3	20. +3	23. −2	26. −3	29. −2
3. +3	6. +2	9. −2	12. +2	15. +3	18. +3	21. +3	24. −3	27. −2	30. +3

TOTAL

ASSESSING YOUR MIND'S WELLNESS

The mind controls all bodily function, including the myriad chemical reactions that occur in every cell. What is on your mind and in your heart can help keep you well or make you ill. Feeling worthy of life brings lightness of heart and inner peace. Sadness and fear weigh heavily on your entire being. Adopting wellness qualities inspires positive thoughts, feelings, and attitudes to reverse illness and support good health.

Knowing others is intelligence. Knowing yourself is true wisdom. Mastering others is strength. Mastering yourself is true power.

LAO-TZU

STRESS is the principal cause of illness in our time. It banishes peace of mind and casts a dim veil over your clearest perceptions.

When you are in a state of stress, its source becomes obscured. Life is challenging, but it is primarily your response and reaction to people and events that causes feelings of stress. People with a strong sense of being able to cope well with life have low levels of stress. Assessing the energy balance of your mind will help you spotlight areas of stress in your life.

Negative feelings and emotions are stress that you impose on yourself. Boulders of anger, resentment, fear, and hurt impede the flow of energy and hinder well-being. Yet the past need not be your prison. It is never too late to heal old wounds.

As you ascend the Pyramid, you will find your life's possibilities and connections. It is a journey to deep wellness through *peace of mind*, the liberation of your *healing force*, and the knowledge that unconditional love is the very source of healing.

WORKING METHOD

Read each statement and check it *only* if it applies to you. If the statement appears only partially applicable, check it if it is *more applicable than not*. Identify the score for each of your checked statements, calculate your total score, and write it in the box. **Important Note** *Make sure to cover up the scorecard while you work through each questionnaire.*

HAPPINESS QUESTIONNAIRE

Happiness is the enriching quality of embracing life with an open heart. Its source is inner contentment, rather than possessions. Happiness expands when you have someone to love or care for, something to hope for, and something to create.

1. I wake up in the morning feeling excited about the coming day.
2. I feel unwanted, unappreciated, and misunderstood.
3. I enjoy my work.
4. I have good friends with whom I enjoy spending time.
5. I worry constantly.
6. I am proud of my family.
7. Simple things in life give me pleasure.
8. I feel best when I am shopping.
9. I get frequent headaches.
10. I'm a genuinely happy person.
11. I feel that the universe is basically unfriendly.
12. A starry night is a thing of beauty.
13. My possessions mean the world to me.
14. I sleep very well.
15. In the recent past, I have contemplated suicide.
16. I feel that I am a lucky person.

17. I don't fear growing older.
18. I smile often and love to laugh.
19. I am embarrassed by my family.
20. There are so many bad things happening in the world that it's hard to be happy.
21. I hug my loved ones often.
22. I fret a lot about things I've done or should have done.
23. My attitude is, if things are going well, then watch out.
24. People come to me to be cheered up.
25. I often feel angry for no reason.
26. I wish I had a more honest relationship with my partner.
27. I'd rather be happy than right.
28. If I let people really know me, I wouldn't be loved.
29. I'd see a glass as half full, rather than half empty.
30. I feel that life is a wonderful adventure.

SCORECARD

1. +3	4. +3	7. +2	10. +3	13. −1	16. +1	19. −2	22. −2	25. −2	28. −2
2. −3	5. −3	8. −1	11. −3	14. +2	17. +2	20. −2	23. −2	26. +2	29. +2
3. +2	6. +2	9. −1	12. +3	15. −3	18. +3	21. +2	24. +2	27. +3	30. +3

TOTAL

KINDNESS & EMPATHY QUESTIONNAIRE

Kindness and empathy are the enriching qualities of recognizing and respecting the sacredness of all life. Kindness and empathy mean accepting and honoring the unique needs of other people with loving sensitivity and heartfelt sincerity.

1. I enjoy helping people who need help.
2. I get grouchy when I have to wait in line.
3. I am generally a warm and caring person.
4. I carry grudges and find it virtually impossible to forgive.
5. I really *do* help little old ladies cross streets.
6. I'm extremely critical of other people.
7. I see God's presence in others.
8. I take time to listen to others' problems.
9. I enjoy making others smile.
10. I believe that it's better to give than to receive.
11. Children are very comfortable with me.
12. I rarely volunteer for good causes.
13. People say they can always rely on me.
14. I find it difficult to say that I'm sorry or admit that I've been wrong.
15. I often commit random acts of kindness.

16. I believe that it's every man for himself.
17. I'm capable of profound compassion.
18. When a salesperson doesn't say "Thank you," I get angry or annoyed.
19. I enjoy teaching others to help themselves.
20. I am sensitive to other people's body language.
21. I'm known as a peacemaker.
22. I usually notice when other people in my life are not feeling well, or have something bothering them.
23. When there is darkness, I try to bring light.
24. I can tell when my spouse or partner or other family members need my special attention or care and readily offer it.

SCORECARD

1. +3	4. −3	7. +3	10. +3	13. +2	16. −3	19. +2	22. +2
2. −1	5. +2	8. +2	11. +2	14. −2	17. +3	20. +1	23. +3
3. +3	6. −2	9. +2	12. −1	15. +3	18. −2	21. +2	24. +2

TOTAL

LEARNING QUESTIONNAIRE

Learning is the enriching quality of gaining wisdom and building character. It means broadening your knowledge, developing skills, and becoming aware of your life's purpose. Learning is the fulfillment of your inquiring nature and potential.

1. Compassion and character are at least as important as knowledge.
2. I visit the library regularly.
3. I don't really need to learn anything new.
4. I enjoy researching what I don't know.
5. I don't keep up with current events.
6. I often look up words in a dictionary.
7. I'd choose a sensitive, touching, inspiring movie over one that is violent, insensitive, or demeaning.
8. I actually enjoy reading the classics.
9. I believe that education is just for young people.
10. Reading is very important to me.
11. I play a musical instrument.
12. I spend most of my spare time watching television.
13. I enjoy visiting museums.
14. Going to a bookstore is fun for me.
15. I hardly ever read.
16. I enjoy traveling to new places.
17. The sights and sounds of nature are not very important to me.
18. If I watch television, it's usually an educational or cultural program.
19. Going to a symphony, a concert, or the ballet is exciting to me.
20. Education should help us distinguish between what is fleeting and what is permanent.
21. I have at least one creative hobby.
22. No amount of training or education could help me.
23. I enjoy taking on new responsibilities and learning new skills.
24. Integrity, values, and ethics are extremely important to me.
25. I generally view failures as opportunities to learn.
26. I very much enjoy good art.
27. I seek out mentors.

SCORECARD

1. +3	4. +2	7. +2	10. +3	13. +2	16. +3	19. +2	22. −3	25. +3
2. +2	5. −2	8. +3	11. +2	14. +2	17. −2	20. +3	23. +3	26. +2
3. −3	6. +2	9. −2	12. −2	15. −2	18. +2	21. +3	24. +3	27. +3

TOTAL

SELF-ESTEEM QUESTIONNAIRE

Self-esteem is the enriching quality of having confidence in the strength and goodness of your soul. It is inspired by faith in your inner self that liberates you from fear. Self-esteem means feeling worthy of life and of being connected to the world.

1. I know I can cope with whatever comes up.
2. I'm uncomfortable at social events, and I avoid them.
3. Change can be exciting.
4. I often feel inadequate.
5. I'm embarrassed by how I look.
6. I am proud of what I have accomplished in my life.
7. I have many flaws that prevent me from being happy.
8. I will speak up in a meeting if I have a question or suggestion.
9. I never vote: my opinion couldn't possibly matter.
10. When I'm speaking to someone, I make a lot of eye contact.
11. I would do anything to get out of having to make a speech or presentation.
12. If I were out of a job, I could quite easily get another one.
13. Important people make me nervous.
14. I am very critical of myself.
15. I enjoy making presentations or speeches.
16. My boss and I have a good relationship.

17. I sometimes think that other people are making fun of me.
18. I smile a lot.
19. My confidence is easily shaken.
20. I'm a good listener.
21. Other people usually know more than I do, so I don't speak up.
22. I often say something stupid.
23. I feel that one person can't change the world.
24. I enjoy helping others.
25. I need a lot of recognition from others to feel good about myself.
26. My parents told me I would never amount to anything, and they were right.
27. At work, I like to spread the praise around.
28. I'm uncomfortable with strangers.
29. I enjoy working with a team of people.
30. I know I am not perfect, but I do very well with what I have.

SCORECARD

1. +3	4. –2	7. –3	10. +2	13. –1	16. +2	19. –2	22. –2	25. –2	28. –1
2. –1	5. –2	8. +2	11. –1	14. –2	17. –1	20. +2	23. –2	26. –3	29. +1
3. +2	6. +3	9. –2	12. +3	15. +1	18. +2	21. –2	24. +2	27. +2	30. +3

TOTAL

ETHICS QUESTIONNAIRE

Ethics is the enriching quality of listening to the voice of your conscience and to the whisper of your heart, which distinguish right from wrong. Ethics means applying the soul's wisdom to your daily life, and ever striving to attain the highest good.

1. If I make a mistake, I freely admit it.
2. If everyone is cheating, I might as well cheat, too.
3. I believe in facing my faults and dealing with them.
4. I'll lie on a résumé, job application, or in an interview.
5. If someone tells me a secret, I would never tell anyone else.
6. I don't steal.
7. My motto is: it's only wrong if you get caught.
8. Others trust my integrity.
9. I try to teach my children to know right from wrong.
10. If my boss asked me to do something that I thought was dishonest, I would not do it.
11. If a salesperson gives me the wrong change in my favor, I keep it. It's not my problem.
12. In this world, it's a waste of time to worry about right and wrong.
13. If I were to make a mistake in an ethical situation, I'd rather be too ethical than possibly do something that might be wrong.
14. If I were to find a wallet on the street with $600 cash in it, I would do everything possible to find the right owner.
15. When filling out an expense report at work, I put down more expenses than I actually had.
16. If my credit card company refunded me twice for an item I returned, I would notify them of their mistake.
17. If my child were to shoplift, I would make him or her take back the item to the store, apologize, and accept the consequences.
18. If I were to find a wallet on the street with $14 cash in it, I would do everything possible to find the right owner.
19. I feel ethics are situational: it all depends.
20. Big companies have lots of money, so it's all right to steal from them if you can get away with it.
21. There are so many unethical people in this world, it's not worth being ethical.
22. I never go back on my word.
23. I am eager to do good, and to be good.
24. It's OK to cheat or steal if you've had a tough life.
25. If I've agreed to do something, I follow through.

SCORECARD

1. +3	4. −3	7. −3	10. +3	13. +3	16. +3	19. −2	22. +3	25. +2
2. −3	5. +2	8. +2	11. −3	14. +3	17. +3	20. −3	23. +2	
3. +2	6. +3	9. +3	12. −3	15. −3	18. +3	21. −3	24. −3	

TOTAL

ASSESSING YOUR SPIRIT'S WELLNESS

Our entire universe is simply a wave of energy. From the tiniest atomic particle to the densest substance known, all life exists within this wave of energy that ebbs and flows in the great sea of being. Spirituality involves perceiving this sea as the source of all goodness and embracing it as the fullness of God. Being in a state of wellness opens your heart to the revelation that through love you are connected to every living thing.

Some day we shall harness the energies of Love. Then, for the second time in the history of the world, Man will have discovered fire.

TEILHARD DE CHARDIN

FAVORING science and ignoring spirituality has always ended in dilemma. Now, it is greater than at any other time in history.

Poets today liken our world to *a spiritual kindergarten that is inhabited by children trying to spell "God" with the wrong blocks.* Yet spirituality and science go hand in hand, since the purpose of good science is surely to *explain* and *apply* the laws of nature to advance humanity. Assessing the wellness of your spirit reminds you of your deepest healing resources.

Every fiber of every human being is invested with a search for meaning and purpose in order eventually to return to the Source of Life. When you recognize yourself as a spiritual being having a human experience, you find ways to overcome feelings of separateness and isolation.

This revives your Healing Force, and transforms the credo *Love One Another* into a way of life. After all, the human miracle is not to fly with wings, or walk on water, but to live with love, in harmony and peace.

WORKING METHOD

Read each statement and check it *only* if it applies to you. If the statement appears only partially applicable, check it if it is *more applicable than not.* Identify the score for each of your checked statements, calculate your total score, and write it in the box. **Important Note** *Make sure to cover up the scorecard while you work through each questionnaire.*

HARMLESSNESS QUESTIONNAIRE

Harmlessness is the elevating state of being kind towards all living things. It means being nonjudgmental, and helping those who are needy. It means being a person others can trust without question, and not hurting your own self in any way.

1. I would not purposely hurt any other living thing.
2. Earth and its creatures exist solely for the use and benefit of humankind.
3. I give kindness with a glad heart to every living creature.
4. It is hard for me to be kind to someone who treats me unkindly.
5. Everyone brings their own special gift to the world.
6. I enjoy arguing just for the sake of it.
7. I see beauty in all of the earth's creatures.
8. I count to ten when I get angry, before I respond.
9. I don't participate in idle gossip.
10. I don't care what other people think of me as long as I get what I want.
11. Silence is often the best way to still the restlessness of my heart.
12. I want to make a positive impact on society.
13. Nice people don't get ahead in this world.
14. I believe that life is sacred.
15. If you treat people as if they were what they ought to be, you help them become what they are capable of being.
16. I've got too much to do in my own life to waste energy on others.
17. I am readily able to apologize, and to accept the apology of other people, and then move on.
18. I'll go out of my way to avoid stepping on flowers.
19. I have done things for which I will never forgive myself.
20. It is important to love and honor the elderly.
21. You don't have to step on others' toes to get ahead.
22. Everyone deserves forgiveness, even people who have caused you pain.
23. Basically, I don't trust anyone.
24. I look for the best in others.
25. Being true to myself is more important than what other people think of me.
26. I take personal responsibility to help protect the environment.
27. Great people are those who do not abuse others.
28. There are people that I just cannot, **and will not**, forgive.
29. Proving myself better than others is not important to me.
30. I treat others as I would wish to be treated myself.

SCORECARD

1. +3	4. −1	7. +3	10. −3	13. −2	16. −3	19. −3	22. +3	25. +2	28. −3	
2. −3	5. +2	8. +2	11. +2	14. +3	17. +3	20. +3	23. −3	26. +2	29. +1	
3. +3	6. −1	9. +2	12. +2	15. +2	18. +3	21. +2	24. +2	27. +2	30. +3	

TOTAL

AWARENESS QUESTIONNAIRE

Awareness is the elevating state of regarding yourself as a spiritual being. It means knowing that your body, in interaction with your mind, is the haven for your soul while on earth. Awareness means putting your heart into everything you do.

1. As I grow older, I seem to notice and admire the color and beauty of the world more.
2. I don't feel particularly connected to the world around me.
3. I recognize and honor the spirit within me.
4. I feel terribly empty and alone.
5. I feel a sacred presence in every moment, everywhere.
6. Every person's smallest contribution can help protect the environment.
7. Much of my life leaves me feeling unfulfilled.
8. Hard work gives me a sense of purpose and fulfillment.
9. I enjoy growing or making things.
10. I meet life's challenges with enthusiasm and courage.
11. I endeavor to understand other people's viewpoints.
12. Life is essentially meaningless.
13. True beauty begins within.
14. Youth is intrinsically more beautiful than age.
15. I believe that when you die, that's it.
16. My sole purpose is to be loving.

17. I'm generally unaware of how people feel unless they tell me.
18. Even-mindedness in all situations is a precious personal treasure.
19. Without sorrow, it would be difficult to appreciate joy.
20. Life fills me with wonder, amazement, and awe.
21. I believe in my own goodness and inner strength.
22. I never trust intuition, only logic and reason.
23. I'm aware that many of the faults I resent in others are often the faults that are present in me.
24. We are here to add what we can to life, not to get what we can from it.
25. We can never fully measure the impact of our actions on others – thus, on the world.
26. If I had a million dollars, then I could be happy.
27. We are a continuation of our ancestors' destiny: ours is a mission of greater endeavor, further striving, and growth.
28. I care for my body as the home of my soul.
29. I believe that death is the soul's return to its source.
30. The true magic of life is its mystery.

SCORECARD

1. +2	4. –3	7. –2	10. +2	13. +2	16. +3	19. +2	22. –2	25. +2	28. +3
2. –2	5. +3	8. +2	11. +2	14. –2	17. –2	20. +3	23. +2	26. 0	29. +2
3. +3	6. +2	9. +2	12. –3	15. –1	18. +3	21. +3	24. +2	27. +2	30. +3

TOTAL

LOVINGNESS QUESTIONNAIRE

Lovingness is the elevating state of knowing that you are connected to all that is, was, and ever will be. It comes with realizing a divine presence in every living thing, equally and impartially. This sacred knowledge is the breath of life.

1. Love is the breath of life.
2. People do not consider me to be a kind and loving person.
3. I'd rather spend quiet time with a loved one than do anything else.
4. Every time I have loved someone, they have used or hurt me.
5. When someone disagrees with me, I often get angry or upset.
6. My relationships with my family, friends, and other loved ones are my greatest source of joy.
7. There will always be war: conflict is natural.
8. Money is meaningless if you don't have love.
9. Love is highly over-rated in this world.
10. I feel goodwill and compassion towards all people.
11. My life is filled with people I care about.
12. Love brings only pain and sorrow.
13. I try to avoid people who are mean-spirited.
14. When there is love in my heart, other people seem to respond positively.
15. I love my nearest and dearest more than I did yesterday, but not as much as I will love them tomorrow.

16. I often judge people too hastily.
17. I am not harboring resentment towards anyone.
18. Love is the greatest healer of all.
19. We cannot be truly loving until we give up envy and hatred.
20. I don't have to tell my family I love them – they know already.
21. The sign of ultimate wisdom is infinite love.
22. I believe that God is Love. Really.
23. My life is so full that I always have something to give others.
24. If love exists, I still haven't found it.
25. I'm unable to love without expecting anything in return.
26. After quarreling with a friend, I'd depend on love and kindness, rather than logic, to restore our friendship.
27. I have trouble expressing loving feelings.
28. Loneliness and feeling unwanted is the most terrible poverty.
29. I try to infuse my life with love.
30. I pray that people everywhere have peace and plenty.

SCORECARD

1. +3	4. −2	7. −1	10. +3	13. +1	16. −1	19. +3	22. +3	25. −2	28. +3
2. −2	5. −2	8. +2	11. +3	14. +2	17. +3	20. −1	23. +3	26. +2	29. +3
3. +2	6. +3	9. −2	12. −3	15. +3	18. +3	21. +3	24. −2	27. −1	30. +3

TOTAL

FAITH & DEVOTION QUESTIONNAIRE

Faith and devotion are the elevating states of being dutiful to the highest good, and inspired by this sacred ideal. Faith and devotion mean consciously striving to live each and every moment of life bathed in the inner light of goodness and truth.

1. Everything happens for a reason: with patience and calm, understanding will come.
2. I believe praying is silly and only for children.
3. I never lose hope.
4. I believe that miracles do happen.
5. I pray only when I'm in trouble, or when someone I love is in trouble.
6. There is a "sacred sculptor" with a universal plan for humankind.
7. I believe that you can achieve virtually anything if you have faith.
8. Adversity builds character and gives a person inner strength.
9. I'd probably have more fun if I weren't worried about God's wrath.
10. I believe that spiritual matters are particularly relevant nowadays.
11. Prayer keeps me in touch with my purpose and inner spirit.
12. I think about God only on religious days and holidays.
13. I believe that life on this earth is merely a preparation.
14. Misfortune is God's way of punishing people.
15. I can find peace and spirituality in work and in simple tasks.
16. I believe God's presence is in every living thing.
17. My problems are much greater than my will to overcome them.
18. One must listen for, trust, and attend to the whisper of one's heart.
19. My goal is peace of mind: pleasure is fleeting.
20. I'll disobey my conscience if it contradicts my desires.
21. Every person has a mission to make something in this world better.
22. Ultimately, goodness and truth will triumph over evil.
23. It's important to love and honor one's parents, even if they are old and appear foolish.
24. There can't be a kind and loving God with all the bad things that happen in this world.
25. True religion seeks justice, peace, and love.
26. I believe that God loves me.
27. I pray more days than not.
28. Physical labor is basically demeaning, or indicative of a lower class.
29. I don't care how I'm remembered after I'm gone.
30. I believe that life is a spiritual pilgrimage.

SCORECARD

1. +3	4. +2	7. +3	10. +2	13. +1	16. +3	19. +2	22. +2	25. +3	28. −2
2. −3	5. −1	8. +3	11. +3	14. −2	17. −3	20. −3	23. +2	26. +3	29. −2
3. +3	6. +3	9. −2	12. −2	15. +2	18. +3	21. +2	24. −2	27. +2	30. +3

TOTAL

TRANSCENDENCE & JOY QUESTIONNAIRE

Transcendence and joy are the elevating states of attaining balance, harmony, and peace of mind by reaching beyond pain and desire. Transcendence and joy mean being overwhelmed by the knowledge of God's love made manifest on earth.

1. It is essential to be truthful.
2. The wonder of my life makes its journey a glorious adventure.
3. I constantly dwell on things I've done, worrying about whether they were the right things.
4. Life is too short not to live every moment to its fullest.
5. I'm usually too busy or tired to be joyful.
6. I often feel overwhelmed by the beauty around me.
7. The sacredness of life is beyond words.
8. Joy is really mostly for children.
9. Worry is never of benefit.
10. My life has no particular purpose.
11. Life's pressures often get me down.
12. Beautiful music can move me to tears.
13. I often wonder whether anyone cares about or even notices me.
14. I believe that surrender to God is the highest form of freedom.
15. I believe joy comes from the simplest things in life.
16. You work hard, do the best you can, and then you die: that's all there is.

17. Giving joy to others fills me with happiness.
18. Material objects may bring pleasure, but true joy comes from within.
19. The painful memories of my past make joy in the future highly improbable.
20. As difficult as things may get, I never give up.
21. I often feel upset when my prayers are not answered as I would wish.
22. Life is serious: it's not meant to be fun.
23. I have a major chronic physical disease or disability, but my heart still sings with joy, hope, and peace.
24. I trust in a higher power.
25. I have deep reverence for life.
26. I feel as if I've lost control over my life and feelings.
27. I feel joyful whenever I think of God.
28. I'm not afraid of growing older.
29. I'd do anything to avoid being alone.
30. My peace of mind comes through being kind, compassionate, loving, and forgiving.

SCORECARD

1. +3	4. +3	7. +3	10. −2	13. −2	16. −2	19. −3	22. −2	25. +3	28. +2
2. +3	5. −2	8. −2	11. −1	14. +3	17. +3	20. +3	23. +3	26. −3	29. −2
3. −3	6. +3	9. +2	12. +2	15. +2	18. +3	21. −3	24. +3	27. +3	30. +3

TOTAL

ENERGY BALANCE SCALES

Completing the questionnaires encourages you to make a nonjudgmental analysis of yourself and your relationship with the world. Your personal profile is here revealed in scales that measure the energy balance of your body, mind, and spirit, and of your whole being.

BODY

MIND

NUTRITION	EXERCISE	HYGIENE & SAFETY	DE-MEDICATION	DE-ADDICTION	HAPPINESS	KINDNESS & EMPATHY	LEARNING	SELF-ESTEEM	ETHICS
40	40	50	40	30	40	40	40	30	50
32	32	40	32	24	32	32	32	24	40
24	24	30	24	18	24	24	24	18	30
16	16	20	16	12	16	16	16	12	20
8	8	10	8	6	8	8	8	6	10
0	0	0	0	0	0	0	0	0	0
–8	–8	–10	–8	–6	–8	–8	–8	–6	–10
–16	–16	–20	–16	–12	–16	–16	–16	–12	–20

Wellness is the graceful dance
of body, mind, and spirit
in tune with each other.

EDWARD A. TAUB, M.D.

YOUR PERSONAL PROFILE

To find your personal profile, first mark your scores from each of the fifteen questionnaires on their appropriate scales. Add together your five scores for each aspect of BODY and mark this sum on the TOTAL body scale below. Do the same for your MIND scores, then for your SPIRIT scores. This clearly identifies whether your energy is in balance, out of balance, or between the two – energy balance disturbed. Then read *Interpreting Your Score* on pages 46 and 47 to understand what your score means.

SPIRIT

HARMLESSNESS	AWARENESS	LOVINGNESS	FAITH & DEVOTION	TRANSCENDENCE & JOY
50	50	50	50	50
40	40	40	40	40
30	30	30	30	30
20	20	20	20	20
10	10	10	10	10
0	0	0	0	0
–10	–10	–10	–10	–10
–20	–20	–20	–20	–20

TOTALS

BODY	MIND	SPIRIT
200	200	250
ENERGY IN BALANCE		
160	160	200
ENERGY BALANCE DISTURBED		
120	120	150
80	80	100
ENERGY OUT OF BALANCE		
40	40	50
0	0	0
–40	–40	–50
–80	–80	–100

INTERPRETING YOUR SCORE

The balance of positive and negative factors affecting body, mind, and spirit represents wellness energy. This energy strives to maintain harmony and well-being. The questionnaires illumine your innate goodness. They reveal areas of energy imbalance, and determine what factors in your life may be causing it. Now find out what your score means by reading the text below the heading here that corresponds to your level on the Energy Balance Scales.

ENERGY IN BALANCE

What lies behind us, and what lies before us, are tiny matters compared to what lies within us. RALPH WALDO EMERSON

Energy in balance means that your energy flows freely. Your natural Healing Force is empowered to support your whole being, protecting and nourishing you. This dynamic equilibrium is cultivated and enhanced by your own high level of personal responsibility.

You are a person of inner strength and conviction who understands the power of your choices. You value yourself and have reverence for life. You are physically active. You eat appropriately. Harmful addictions and risky behavior are not a part of your life.

You feel the universe is basically friendly and have confidence in your ability to cope well with most life situations. You do not act in ways that conflict with or violate your values and integrity. You are a person that others respect, admire, and revere. You will find it easy to make any positive changes needed in order to reach even higher levels of wellness.

Signposts of Balance

- You demonstrate the credo, *Love One Another,* in every aspect of your life.
- You have a sense of mission, purpose, and order that enables you to put your beliefs into practice.
- You strive to be fully present in the here and now, neither dwelling on what is past nor unduly fearing for the future.
- You have strong feelings of commitment to your community, and of connectedness to the world.

People travel to wonder at the height of mountains,

at the huge waves of the sea, at the long courses of rivers,

at the vast compass of the ocean, at the circular motion of the stars …

And they pass by themselves without wondering.

ST. AUGUSTINE, AN EARLY THEOLOGIAN

ENERGY BALANCE DISTURBED

Inspiration, creative power, and energy flow into you when you attune yourself to the Infinite. PARAMAHANSA YOGANANDA

Energy balance disturbed means that your energy flow is impeded. Your natural Healing Force has become suppressed, but is striving to restore energy balance.

Millions like you belong to the "walking wounded" and "worried well." Fortunately, your potential to be well is great. Achieving a score at this level indicates that you have been taking *some* responsibility for your well-being, but have neglected your *whole self*.

You have a sufficiently high regard for life to want to look and feel good. Greater efforts to care for your body, mind, *and* spirit will empower you to develop higher levels of balanced energy that will fulfill your potential for whole wellness.

Your scores identify areas of concern. These are the factors disturbing your energy balance. Remember that ill-health indicates a lack of love in your life. The key to restoring energy balance is forgiveness and love, for others *and yourself*. Nourishing yourself with kindness and compassion reaps dramatic health rewards.

Signposts of Disturbance
- ∽ You feel a general dissatisfaction with life, and lack a clear purpose, plan, or intent.
- ∽ You seek quick fixes for difficulties, and rarely try to discover the root cause of a problem.
- ∽ You have difficulty controlling bad habits, and allow stress to overcome your resolve.
- ∽ You have weight problems, exercise infrequently, and prefer to avoid challenge.

ENERGY OUT OF BALANCE

If you were to take just one step towards God, God would take one thousand steps towards you. SATHYA SAI BABA

Energy out of balance means that your energy flow is blocked. While struggling to maintain balance, your natural Healing Force has been overcome. This is why energy out of balance eventually becomes disease.

Do not despair. Fear not. And never give in. Even the smallest efforts to revive your Healing Force can yield a harvest of healthful wellness energy to restore harmony and balance. It is never too late to take the very first step towards better self-care.

Your scores in all areas indicate that you have low self-esteem. This is reflected in your lifestyle, and in the choices you make. Pursuing this familiar path will just hasten your body's natural decline and accelerate the appearance of disease.

Your health and happiness now require a sustained and concentrated effort. Build strength and enhance your attitude by taking immediate steps to change at least some of your unhealthful answers into healthful ones. Just simple acts of kindness, towards others *but especially towards yourself*, can give you the necessary boost to recognize your unlimited healing potential.

Signposts of Disharmony
- ∽ You feel that the universe is basically unfriendly, and that your life is out of control.
- ∽ You are enslaved by alcohol, tobacco, or drugs.
- ∽ You experience prolonged periods of gloom and despondency, and rarely see lightness in life.
- ∽ You cause yourself and others deliberate hurt.

WELLNESS A

CTION PLAN

PYRAMID OF HUMAN ASPIRATION

The Pyramid of Human Aspiration symbolizes the place where the Divine touches the earth. It is the place where the Infinite and Absolute reaches out to embrace and enfold you in health, happiness, and love. Here is the point where your life connects with the great sea of life. Here is where the human ensemble of body, mind, and spirit is infused with energy from the eternal Source of All Energy.

HUMAN life springs forth from an explosive point of energy that becomes substance. Each tiny seed of life-energy contains all the resources, gifts, and talents of the adult human being.

New life grows and is kept safe within the nurture of its mother's womb. The moment of separation occurs when the child is born and for the first time experiences itself as a unique and separate being.

From this time forward, human life becomes what we know it to be, deep in our hearts: a spiritual pilgrimage back to the Source of

PYRAMIDS AT GIZA, EGYPT
The moving spirit of aspiration, ingenuity, and challenge is embodied in these mighty resting places of the ancient Pharaohs.

the Infinite Energy from which we came. Thus, the journey of life and our purpose in life entail *identifying*, *aspiring to*, and ever *striving towards* an Infinite and Eternal Ideal.

This Ideal is defined in Platonic wisdom as a prime mover that does not move, an entity without form that has breathed life into us, and a being without substance that yet exists in every living thing.

REUNION WITH THE INFINITE
The Pyramid of Human Aspiration enables us to regain a sense of our completeness, and re-establish our connections with life. It nurtures every part of our being, just as we were nurtured in a mother's womb, and gives us all that we require to make the journey to self-healing.

PHYSICAL WELLNESS

The body is the *substance* of the human ensemble. It is an intricate mechanism that translates the energy of the mind into activity and action.

The body's ability to regulate, repair, and control its function is supported by the power of the Healing Force.

Good nutrition and regular amounts of moderate exercise allow the energy of the body to flow freely. This enables the body to care for itself, and to build the reserves of physical energy needed during times of illness and stress.

Physical wellness is the foundation of the Pyramid of Human Aspiration. It is attained when the energy of the body is balanced within itself. It is maintained when the energy of the body is attuned to the energy of both mind and spirit.

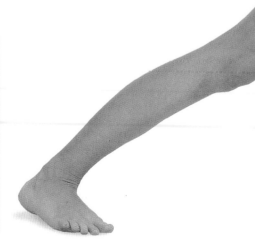

When you are inspired by some great purpose,
all your thoughts break their bonds: your
mind transcends limitations, and you find
yourself in a new, great, and wonderful world.

PATANJALI, FATHER OF YOGA

MENTAL WELLNESS

The mind is the *inner eye* of the human
ensemble. Its myriad complex processes
transform the energy of the spirit into
thoughts, feelings, and ideas.

The mind's ability to think, wonder,
and reflect elevates human beings from
other members of the animal world.

Stillness of thought and the absence
of harmful addictions allow the energy
of the mind to flow freely. This releases
energy for creativity and learning, and
the ingenuity needed to reach beyond
apathy and face life's challenge.

Mental wellness lies at the heart of
the Pyramid of Human Aspiration.
Its motivating force is the
eternal flame of
Remembered
Wellness.

SPIRITUAL WELLNESS

The spirit is the *divine inspiration* of the
human ensemble. Each and every cell is
invested with the energy of the spirit. It
is this that fuses the energy of mind and
body into one meaning and purpose.

The spirit's ability to recognize the
sacred presence in all life compels the
mind in its striving towards the Ideal.

Faith, love, and surrender allow the
energy of the spirit to flow freely. This
empowers the essential change needed
to bring the energy of body, mind, and
spirit into perfect balance.

Spiritual wellness soars at the summit
of the Pyramid of Human Aspiration. It
defines the path and shines light on the
aim. It is both substance and essence. It
is both journey and goal – the ultimate
security of rediscovering Love the Ideal.

◁ THE WARRIOR POSE
*The practice of yoga strives to bring body,
mind, and spirit into equilibrium in order to
restore health and maintain balance. This
dynamic position, in which the whole body
reaches upwards from a firm base, creates
feelings of empowerment and strength.*

SEVEN STEPS TO WELLNESS

Energy is the seed, the root, the flower of all life. Human energy is a unique thread, woven into the fabric of the entire universe. When energy is out of balance, dis-ease results. Ascending the Pyramid of Human Aspiration restores balance. To attain the point of balance – the point where pain, worry, and turbulence dissolve into a harmonious equilibrium of body, mind, and spirit – it is necessary to rise through each of the seven steps.

HUMAN BEINGS are aspirational beings. We all aspire to what is true, what is beautiful, and what is good – we aspire to Love. Our common purpose involves us in a continual striving after that Ideal. In the physical world of substance, in the worlds of our senses and of what can be described, everything changes with time. Yet the Ideal is timeless – infinite, unchangeable.

Abandoned, even forgotten, the Ideal of infinite and unchangeable Love exists, ingrained within us as inner knowledge of what is right and what is wrong. It is the moral basis of our being, which is forever capable of being rekindled. Stress, worry, and anguish bite deep into Love the Ideal, disrupting health and happiness, impeding the flow of our natural Healing Force, and allowing I-L-L to become our cry and sad expression of I *Lack* Love.

Ascending the Pyramid allows us to rediscover Love and to embrace the natural Healing Force within that is the power to heal diseases and the peace to heal our hearts.

REMEMBERED WELLNESS
Everyone has the ability to stoke up the flame of their own Healing Force and to attain the summit of the Pyramid – there, Remembered Wellness reigns, time without end.

Everyone has the ability to attain the lofty point where the energies of body and mind and spirit are so attuned that distinctions between them vanish. Only baby steps and persistence are needed. No greater effort is required than the courage of an infant learning to walk. The Roman philosopher, Seneca, said: *It is not because things are difficult that we do not dare; it is because we do not dare that they are difficult.*

BIG OAK FROM LITTLE ACORN
Human energy springs forth from the same source that coordinates the dance of the seasons and holds heaven and earth in balance. Rooted in the rich soil of a grassy hillside, this sturdy oak tree embodies the energy encapsulated in its seed. Just so is it within you to create exceptional changes from the very smallest of beginnings.

STEP SEVEN – REDISCOVERING LOVE

Forever true, forever beautiful, forever good – Love is the Ideal. Given freely and without condition, love causes the soul to sing with joy. Give all to love.

Beneath illness lies a longing for love. Nothing affects wellness more deeply than love. The song of the soul is vital to bring balance and wellness into life.

IN PERFECT BALANCE
Yin and yang – complementary yet opposing principles – illustrate the eternal and unchangeable Ideal.

SYMBOL OF INNOCENCE
Peace flows through body, mind, and spirit whenever forgiveness is extended with an open, unencumbered heart.

STEP SIX – REACHING FORGIVENESS

Forgiveness heals sorrows and wounds. Most people want to be understood and appreciated – forgiving them does not mean allowing injustice to occur.

Forgiveness is heartfelt compassion for oneself and for others that occurs with seeing the sacredness in life. It requires a willingness to be happy, not right.

STEP FIVE – BUILDING SELF-ESTEEM

Self-esteem reflects feelings of personal worthiness. These feelings are more a consequence of current behavior than an outgrowth of fortune or misfortune.

What is done today, using the gifts of heart and mind, is what matters most. Personal integrity and ethical behavior are the best barometers of self-esteem.

FULL CIRCLE
True purpose is revealed as self-esteem merges into a knowledge of the inner self.

STEP FOUR – DE-ADDICTION

Addictions – particularly nicotine and alcohol – are all energy thieves. These harmful substances disrupt the balance and impede the flow of natural energy.

Addictions injure the body, harm the mind, and suppress the exuberance of the human spirit. They ruin not only health and happiness, but life itself.

LEAFY GLADE
Turbulent thoughts and feverish desires can be released in tranquil places, giving the body ease from stress.

STEP THREE – MEDITATION

Meditation is the process by which the mind is brought into the here and now, calming our mental storms, uncovering an inner source of clarity and stillness.

In meditating, one sits in the presence of peace. Meditation strengthens the body against the punishment of stress and reveals the doorway into the soul.

QUIET CONTEMPLATION
Following an everyday program of yoga and meditation creates a strong body and a disciplined mind.

STEP TWO – ENJOYABLE EXERCISE

Exercise is an absolute requirement for balanced energy and health. The best kind of exercise is activity that makes one breathe faster, and smile as well.

A sense of playfulness helps. Even the smallest increase in physical activity will lower stress and the risks of heart attacks, cancer, diabetes, and stroke.

STEP ONE – EINSTEIN ENERGY DIET

Food either contributes to, or detracts from, the balance of the human energy system. Food is nourishment for both body and mind – nurture for the spirit.

To support wellness and harmony, it is essential to become aware of the kind of food one eats; to prepare it with love; and to eat it mindfully and soulfully.

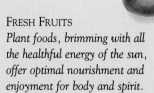

FRESH FRUITS
Plant foods, brimming with all the healthful energy of the sun, offer optimal nourishment and enjoyment for body and spirit.

ASCENDING THE PYRAMID

TO ASCEND the Pyramid of Human Aspiration is to reach into the heart of the relationship between physical pain, mental worry, and spiritual commotion. Each of its seven steps is equivalent to a major ingredient in a physician's prescription for lifetime wellness. Each step is necessary for the prescription to be effective. No step is more or less important than any other. Healing is not an *event*. It is a *process* that demands a sustained effort and commitment to overcome indecision and inertia.

The seven steps of the Pyramid can be likened to the seven colors of a rainbow. Each color of the rainbow is beautiful in its own right, yet the true brilliance and splendor of the rainbow is the sum of all its colors in concert with each other.

In the same way, all seven steps of the Pyramid are integral to the total process of healing. Each step is an ideal in its own right *and it is also* a reflection of the Ideal of the Good – Truth, Beauty, and Love.

LIFETIME WELLNESS

Ascending the Pyramid, by way of the seven steps to self-healing, is a design for a lifetime journey to the Ideal of the Good. Thus, ascending the Pyramid entails striving always towards the Good.

The journey leads to balance and harmony of your physical, mental, and spiritual energy. Scoring in the wellness range across all fifteen of the Energy Balance Scales (pages 44 and 45) is your ultimate goal.

The moment you decide to make the journey, its goal is within your grasp. When wellness is achieved, the eternal source of your strength emerges – your Healing Force that protects, nourishes, and supports your whole being by reviving the spirit of Remembered Wellness. It is a journey with infinite rewards.

There are great moments of wonder as we surrender
to the stream of life force, but the knowledge of who and what
we are often eludes us. What we are, in essence, is all
things, all past time, and the infinite possibility of the future.

RESHAD FEILD

BE WELL – BE WHOLE

Your journey of a lifetime is divided into easily achievable baby steps. It is nevertheless an undertaking that requires serious concentration.

Wherever you are in life you are ascending and what you call results are just beginnings. Therefore, each step that you complete creates the beginning of the next.

Your signature – upon your word of honor – declares your resolve to take personal responsibility for your own health. Begin then with a vow to dedicate yourself to healing, and sign your name to the pledge, with genuine sincerity and sacredness, to set the healing process in motion. Let your heart rejoice to the eternal rhythm of your Healing Force that choruses, *Be well – be whole.*

THREE-DAY PREPARATION

Each step of the Pyramid involves inward as well as upward progress. The following guide helps you lay the essential cornerstones for your lifetime path to wellness.

Nourishment for both body and soul is the universal starting place. Therefore, begin the *Einstein Energy Diet* (page 56) on *day one.* Eat more foods that provide energy and fewer foods that deplete energy. Also take a *wellness walk* (page 96), and make sure you get a bit huffy and puffy.

On *day two*, introduce yourself to a routine of easy *yoga* (page 83) and *meditation* (page 98). Yoga postures, breathing, and ethics will increase your stamina and also add vitality to your wellness walk.

Meditation will start to cultivate a calm and positive outlook. Let go of any lingering resistance you may feel by stilling your thoughts. Focus the energy of your whole being on your dedication to healing.

On *day three*, just continue with the Einstein Energy Diet, wellness walking, easy yoga, and meditation. Your sail is now properly set to fill with the fair wind of wellness, and your lifetime journey has begun.

PERSONAL PLEDGE & COMMITMENT

I proclaim my commitment to ascend the
Pyramid of Human Aspiration by rising
through each one of the seven
steps to self-healing.

❧

I will strive towards the ideal in each step.
I will be guided by integrity & truth.
I will rediscover Love, the Breath of Life.

YOUR SIGNATURE
_____

DATE
_____

WITNESS'S SIGNATURE
_____

EINSTEIN ENERGY DIET

*Food either contributes to, or detracts from, the balance of your energy system.
Food is nourishment for body and mind – nurture for the spirit. To support
wellness and harmony, it is essential to become aware of the kind of food
you eat, to prepare it with love, and to eat it mindfully and soulfully.
Step One identifies the first ideal – a moderate eating plan for life.*

EINSTEIN ENERGY DIET

THE EINSTEIN Energy Diet is a radical concept in eating that acknowledges the discovery of the great physicist, Albert Einstein. It is inspired by nature and grounded in two *laws of thermodynamics*.

Einstein made clear how *energy turns into mass and vice versa*. This means that all life is energy. Food energy turns into the substance of your body and provides fuel for it to function. So you are an energy system that becomes what it eats.

According to the *law of entropy*, all energy systems eventually fall apart. This means that your body will naturally decline with age and return its energy to the Source of all energy. However, you can slow down entropy by eating foods that are full of life-energy – vegetables, fruits, and grains.

Plant foods capture the energy of the sun to slow down entropy. They are steeped in sunlight, and infused with wind, earth, and water. They are the synthesis of life-energy that allows your body to absorb the very rays of the sun. On the other hand, meat and animal products contain little sunlight. They have poor life-energy and only hasten entropy.

The *law of conservation of energy* declares that energy can be neither created nor destroyed. Therefore, if you consume excess food with poor life-energy, your body must either burn off its energy with exercise or convert its energy into fat. This is the major cause of obesity.

Eating is alchemy, the conversion of food into life *and* enjoyment. In this way it becomes possible to eat very well, to lose excess fat, and to maintain a healthy weight forever.

REMEMBER TO EAT MINDFULLY

Gratitude and appreciation help change food into healthful energy and joy. At least put your cares aside for a time, and eat while you are feeling calm. Pause to reflect that your food enables you to see, hear, speak, sing, touch, walk, love, and breathe. Surely this merits a moment of wonder and amazement. This also helps you eat less because you recognize when you have eaten enough. It is truly worth learning to eat with awareness. After all, *what* and *when* and *how* you eat inspires the environment for the birth of all your thoughts, feelings, actions, and ideas.

THIN SPAGHETTI
WITH HERBS

GARLIC
CLOVES

CHOPPED GARLIC

FLATLEAF PARSLEY

MINCED PARSLEY

CRUSHED DRIED
RED CHILI PEPPER

PURE SALT CRYSTALS

USE NATURE'S LIFE-ENERGY TO LOSE FAT – NOT HOPE

DEPRIVATION and hunger are unsatisfactory means of weight loss. The way to lose fat is to eat abundant amounts of foods bursting with nature's life-energy. This gives your body fuel to burn away its excess fat. Life-energy is in food that has grown in the soil, is fresh, and close to its natural form. Processed and refined foods are stripped of most of their useful energy. Regular exercise is also necessary to burn fat. This is the weight loss plan that fills you with life *and* hope.

TORTELLONI WITH PARSLEY

FACTS ABOUT EATING

Your body gathers, assimilates, and stores its energy in rhythm with the rising and setting of the sun. Thus, you function best with high bursts of quick-acting fruit energy in the morning, moderate bursts of energy from vegetables during midday, and lower bursts of long-acting complex carbohydrate energy for your resting hours. Your metabolism will adjust if you must work at night.

If you want to nap after a meal, it is because your own life-energy is being used to digest the foods you have chosen. Can you imagine an automobile not starting as a result of being fueled? Animal products and refined foods use up your own life-energy to digest them – energy that could be used to burn up your excess fat. Therefore, avoid them.

There are numerous misleading myths about food and what, when, and how to eat. Here are essential guidelines for achieving balanced energy and permanent weight loss.

Calculating cholesterol and fat grams is unnecessary.

It's very simple. Only animal foods are a source of harmful cholesterol and fat. Foods filled with life-energy have never had a mother or a face.

Sugar in a candy bar is not the same as sugar in a strawberry.

Fruit is bursting with life-energy but a candy bar is dead. This is why the energy derived from the fat in an avocado is not equivalent to energy from the fat in a strip of bacon. In the same way, fresh orange juice has abundant life-energy while juice from concentrate has little.

Regular bowel movements are important.

Lethargy, discomfort, and disease result when wastes are left for too long in the human energy system. Plant fiber ensures regularity, and decreases cancer risk by half.

Eat a hearty fresh fruit-filled breakfast each day.

Until noon, have all the fresh fruit and fresh fruit juice you wish. Fruit provides more life-energy than any other food and requires almost no energy to digest.

Stay on the top five rungs of the Food Energy Ladder (page 59) for the rest of the day.

During midday, have mostly soups, salads, and whole grain breads. For dinner, add complex carbohydrates like pasta, rice, or potatoes. They provide a long-acting, nourishing release of life-energy to help your body burn excess fat. *Just eat them without meats and rich sauces.*

Avoid eating after 8.00PM.

This will enable you to sleep more soundly and thus store up healthful energy. Adjust this time so that it is two hours before your bedtime if your work schedule necessitates it. Fresh fruit is best if you must snack.

Avoid cow's milk.

Only humans believe they need the milk of another species to maintain good health. Cow's milk is proper nourishment only for baby cows.

FRESH ORANGE WITH ITS JUICE

THE FOOD ENERGY LADDER

THE FOOD ENERGY LADDER shows, in graphic form, the principles of how to eat according to the Ideal – the Einstein Energy Diet (pages 56 and 57). Soulless, mechanical descriptions of food that reduce it to calories, fats, carbohydrates, and proteins are merely ideas contrived by science in order to make comprehensible the laws of nature.

Scientific descriptions of food let misconceptions and myths get in the way of the Ideal. Ideal food looks at food from the perspective of energy. It is energy to preserve physical, mental, and spiritual wellness. Ideal food stimulates our *healing force*, nurtures our spirit, and inspires us to think, feel, and act in ways promoting harmony and balance.

Considering your everyday food as energy brings an entirely different perspective to how you eat. Often we confuse emotional longings for food with the body's signals that it is time to take in energy – fuel for the body to be able to carry out its work. Advertising shapes our food choices and eating patterns. What true hunger feels like passes us by.

Eating live food – food that grows in the soil, that is fresh and close to its natural form – contributes to the efficient energy system that is your body. Because live food gives the body more energy than it uses up during the process of digestion, energy remains available to burn excess fat, to help suppress disease, and to maintain a state of balance.

The Energy Ladder chart helps to identify the foods that are live and thus high in energy, and the foods that deplete energy. Fruit provides more energy than any other food, in part because it takes almost no energy to digest. Flesh foods, and all those on the lower rungs, make you feel sleepy, because they need so much valuable energy to digest.

THE ANIMAL PROTEIN MYTH

You may feel that it is impossible for you to be completely fit and healthy, and have enough energy to sustain a busy life, if you don't have animal protein in your diet. Or you may feel you cannot make satisfying main meals without the focus of meat. You may think you will feel weak if you do not have meat. Or you may simply enjoy meat and not want to give it up.

BLACK-EYED PEAS

BROWN RICE

YELLOW SOYBEANS

SOFT TOFU

FIRM TOFU

SILKEN TOFU

If thoughts similar to these deter you from eating mostly plant foods, remind yourself that the beef we choose to eat for protein comes from cows that get all of their protein from grass. Even elephants and oxen, which are the strongest of earth's animals, eat only plants. Protein from animals is not required for you to remain in good health. Foods from the top five rungs of the Ladder provide every nutrient for perfect balance.

HOW TO USE THE LADDER

Your ideal, ultimate goal is to keep within the upper five rungs of the ladder. Fresh fruits and vegetables, dried legumes, grains, whole grain breads and cereals, nuts, and olive oil provide all of your nutritional requirements. If this way of eating is new for you, you might want to include a moderate amount of fish and poultry – two or three times a week at most – initially. Dabble in the lower rungs with restraint, for all of these foods deplete energy.

- Eat as great a variety of foods on the upper five rungs as you can.
- Aim to avoid everything on the five rungs below Poultry.
- Consume mostly fresh fruits and juices until noon.
- Prepare fresh produce as soon before eating it as is practical.
- Eat joyfully, and in moderation.

△ FRUITS *are Ideal Food – eat as much as you wish. Fresh seasonal produce that is locally grown provides optimal energy.*

FRUITS

△ VEGETABLES *are packed with all the goodness of sun and soil. Eat these colorful energy-givers in abundance.*

VEGETABLES

△ PASTA, RICE, & POTATOES *are slow-burning, efficient fuels that provide sustained energy to help your body to stay well.*

PASTA RICE POTATOES

WHOLE GRAIN BREADS CEREALS

△ WHOLE GRAIN BREADS & CEREALS *are a life-enhancing source of complex carbohydrates.*

NUTS AVOCADOS OLIVE OIL

△ NUTS, AVOCADOS, & OLIVE OIL *contain no cholesterol. They are healthful but rich – enjoy them, but in moderation.*

FISH

△ FISH, *particularly if fresh and free from contaminants, is a healthful alternative to meat if you cannot do without flesh foods.*

POULTRY

△ POULTRY *is less harmful than red meat. Seek out humanely raised birds and avoid eating their skin and fat.*

BEEF PORK LAMB VEAL

△ MEAT *is not Ideal Food. Make a conscious decision to not burden your body and mind with any kind of meat.*

LOW-FAT DAIRY PRODUCTS

△ LOW-FAT DAIRY PRODUCTS *are a more healthful choice than full-fat milk, cheeses, and margarine. Use both low-fat and nonfat varieties with restraint.*

REGULAR DAIRY PRODUCTS

△ REGULAR DAIRY PRODUCTS *make your mucous membranes work overtime, and clog up your system.*

EGGS

△ EGGS *should be an occasional food – try to obtain them fresh, from free-range birds. If you must have eggs, avoid eating the yolks.*

CANDY SWEETS

△ CANDY & SWEETS *do not provide lasting energy. Putting these into your body will sap your vitality and encourage a dull sleepiness.*

EVERYDAY DINING & RECIPES

THIS ENJOYABLE eating plan for life is flexible and infinitely adaptable. It has *three keys* that restore and balance energy and an *added ingredient* that transforms nature's gifts into nourishment for your whole being. The *first key* is to have mostly fresh fruits and juices until noon. The *second key* is to have one meal of mostly vegetables and good bread. The *third key* is to have one hearty meal of vegetables and complex carbohydrates like pasta, rice, or potatoes. The *added ingredient* is love.

Honoring yourself for your choice of food and regarding food with gratitude sets off a subtle adjustment within body and mind that allows you to receive more of the healthful essence of what you are eating. Thus, *what, when,* and *how* you eat is vital for your health.

You can bring the spirit of celebration into everyday eating by taking time to choose the freshest produce, appreciating its fragrance and color. Attune what you eat to the rhythm of your day. Eat to recapture all the goodness and life-energy of the sun. Remember always when eating that the essential *added ingredient* is simply love.

FRESH FRUITS & JUICES UNTIL NOON   SALAD, SOUP, & GOOD BREAD

▽ FROM SUNRISE TO SUNSET
The semicircle is divided into three segments that illustrate which foods are the ideal to eat at different times of day. Be flexible, however. Lunch need not mean noon, but the time you choose to eat a lighter meal. Dinner foods are heartier fare for slow energy-release, and help you rest and relax when your work is done.

SIMPLE POINTERS TO HEALTHFUL EATING

- Look for a reliable source of the freshest fruits and vegetables in your neighborhood. A farmer's market is wonderful for locally grown, seasonal produce.
- Whole grains are a rich source of valuable nutrients and fiber. If you do not usually eat whole grain foods, consider starting with some whole-wheat pasta.
- Add wine sparingly to soups and stews, if you wish, for interest.

- Dried mixtures such as *Herbs of Provence* and *Italian Herbs* are a useful substitute for fresh herbs.
- Use light olive oil if you do not care for the distinctive flavor of the darker product.
- Eat abundant amounts of life-energy food, and also exercise regularly, to help your body burn up excess fat and achieve balance and harmony.
- Eat mindfully – not while you are engaged in other activity.
- The remaining six steps of the Pyramid are *absolutely integral* to the Einstein Energy Diet.

AT LUNCH VEGETABLES & PASTA, RICE, OR POTATOES AT DINNER

A GOOD START TO THE DAY

The first meal of the day needs food that awakens body and mind – brings gladness to the spirit. Fresh fruits are the ideal, full of precious vitamins and minerals, alive with energy and vitality. Choose colors, flavors, and textures that appeal to your sense of pleasure. If it is just not possible to feel satisfied and limit yourself to fruit until noon, then eat some whole grain bread without butter or unsweetened cereal with nonfat milk.

A PLATEFUL OF FRESH FRUITS

SERVES 2

1 small cantaloupe melon, sliced
1 medium mango, sliced
1½ cups (180g) raspberries
1½ cups (180g) blueberries
2 green or purple figs, quartered
sprigs of fresh mint for garnish

∾ Divide the melon and mango slices between two individual serving plates. Arrange half the raspberries and half the blueberries on each of the plates and top with the quartered figs. Garnish with fresh mint.

A PLATEFUL
OF FRESH
FRUITS

FRESH FRUIT SMOOTHIES

Fresh fruits blended together make a quickly prepared boost of energy to get you going. You need not use the fruits suggested here. Choose what is fresh, ripe, in season, and available. If the fruits are not juicy, you may wish to add some spring water.

Melon, Strawberry, & Lime

SERVES 2

2 cups (300g) chopped sweet melon
(cantaloupe or watermelon)
2 cups (300g) chopped strawberries
or raspberries
grated zest and juice of 1 lime
½ cup (125ml) spring water, carbonated or
still (*optional*)
lime slices for garnish

∾ Put the melon, strawberries or raspberries, and lime zest and juice in a blender.

∾ Blend together until smooth. Add the spring water, if using, and blend for another moment. Divide between two glasses. Garnish each with a lime slice and serve immediately.

Mango, Peach, Passion Fruit, & Banana

Serves 2

1 large ripe mango
1 large ripe peach
2 passion fruits
2 bananas, sliced
½ cup (125ml) spring water, carbonated or still (*optional*)
sprigs of fresh mint for garnish

∾ Remove skins from the mango and peach, remove pits, and roughly dice the flesh.

∾ Halve the passion fruits and scoop out the seeds and pulp into a small strainer. Rub and press to extract as much juice as possible.

∾ Put the mango and peach flesh, passion fruit juice, and bananas in a blender.

∾ Blend together until smooth. Add the spring water, if using, and blend for another moment. Divide between two glasses. Garnish each with a sprig of mint and serve immediately.

Apricot, Blueberry, & Orange

Serves 2

2 cups (300g) chopped ripe apricots
or chopped fresh pineapple
1 cup (125g) blueberries
grated zest of ½ orange
1 cup (250ml) fresh orange juice
½ cup (125ml) spring water, carbonated or still (*optional*)
orange slices for garnish

∾ Put the apricots or pineapple, blueberries, and orange zest and juice in a blender.

∾ Blend together until smooth. Add the spring water, if using, and blend for another moment. Divide between two glasses. Garnish each with an orange slice and serve immediately.

BREADS FOR BREAKFAST OR ANY TIME OF DAY
Real bread celebrates the bounty of grain fed with the goodness of the soil, watered and ripened by nature's hand. This hearty sample is a combination of wheat flour, yellow cornmeal, and whole grain oats.

OATMEAL CEREAL

Serves 2

2½ cups (600ml) water
⅓ cup (50g) Irish oatmeal or Scotch oats
1 tablespoon bran
1 tablespoon wheat germ
4 fresh or dried unsweetened dates, pitted
6 dried unsulfured apricots
2 tablespoons raisins (*optional*)
1 tablespoon sunflower seeds
1 tablespoon pumpkin seeds
Nonfat milk for serving (*optional*)

∾ Put the water in a medium saucepan, bring to a boil, sprinkle in the oatmeal, bran, and wheat germ. Stir over medium heat until the mixture starts to boil, lower the heat and simmer, stirring occasionally, until the cereal thickens, about 18 minutes.

∾ Chop the dates and apricots. Add them to the cereal with the raisins, if using, and cook 2–3 minutes longer.

∾ Remove from the heat and stir in the seeds. Serve the cereal with nonfat milk, if desired.

DINING ON THE LIGHT SIDE

Light meals need food that replenishes and sustains energy, providing motivation for work. Grains, pasta, or dried legumes, with abundant amounts of fresh salads and preferably raw vegetables, are the ideal. Avoid flesh foods, which can make you feel sleepy.

GRAIN SALAD

SERVES 4

2 cups (300g) cooked grain, such as millet, quinoa, or rice *or*
2 cups (300g) presoaked couscous or bulgur wheat
6 scallions, trimmed and chopped
1 cup (125g) diced cucumber
1 medium mango, peeled and chopped
½ cup (60g) raisins or golden raisins
½ cup (60g) chopped walnuts
1 large avocado, peeled and chopped
2 tablespoons chopped cilantro
2 tablespoons sesame seeds, toasted
2 tablespoons sunflower seeds, toasted
Lemon Dressing (page 75)
salt and freshly ground black pepper
slices of mango and avocado for garnish (*optional*)

GRAIN SALAD

❧ Put the grain in a large bowl. Add the scallions, cucumber, mango, raisins, walnuts, avocado, cilantro, and toasted seeds. Stir thoroughly to combine all the ingredients. Pour the dressing over the salad. Season lightly or to taste. Toss again, taking great care not to break up the pieces of mango and avocado.

❧ Arrange the grain salad on four individual serving plates. Garnish with slices of mango and avocado, if desired.

EINSTEIN ENERGY SALAD

SERVES 4

2 medium tomatoes, quartered
6 fresh ears of baby corn, halved lengthwise
1 cup (60g) small broccoli florets
1 medium yellow bell pepper, seeded and sliced
2 cups (175g) finely chopped green cabbage
1 cup (90g) finely chopped red cabbage
6 radishes, sliced
1 celery stalk, chopped
1 cup (30g) arugula leaves
2 ripe avocados, peeled and sliced
1 medium carrot, thinly sliced
1 cup (90g) sliced button mushrooms
2 tablespoons pumpkin or sunflower seeds
Lemon Dressing (page 75)
1 tablespoon chopped cilantro
2 tablespoons roughly chopped pistachio nuts

❧ Combine all the prepared vegetables and seeds in a large bowl.

❧ Add the dressing and chopped cilantro and toss lightly. Sprinkle with the pistachio nuts and serve with baked potatoes or bread.

EGGPLANT & TOMATO SANDWICH

SERVES 4

1 medium eggplant (about ½ pound [250g])
4 teaspoons olive oil
1 garlic clove, minced
4 large bread rolls, or 2 Italian ciabatta
1 large beefsteak tomato (about ½ pound [250g]),
thinly sliced
¼ cup (30g) black olives, sliced (*optional*)
½ cup (60g) feta cheese, crumbled (*optional*)
salt and freshly ground black pepper
a few fresh basil leaves
Lemon Dressing (page 75)

➤ Preheat the broiler. Cut the eggplant in slices
¾-inch (2-cm) thick. Brush sides with a little olive
oil. Arrange on a baking sheet, in one layer, and
cook 4-inches (10-cm) from the heat, until the slices
brown. Turn them over, sprinkle with garlic, and
brush with remaining oil. Broil until golden.

➤ Split the rolls in half, or cut the ciabatta in two
and then split. Arrange eggplant slices on the bases,
top with slices of tomato, and sprinkle with olives
and cheese, if using. Season as desired and sprinkle
with torn basil leaves. Drizzle some dressing over the
filling. Replace the roll or bread tops and serve.

AVOCADO SANDWICH

SERVES 4

1 large French baguette or 2 Italian ciabatta
Mustard & Honey Dressing (page 75)
1–2 large beefsteak tomatoes, sliced
1 large ripe avocado, peeled and thinly sliced
½ cucumber, peeled and sliced
1 cup (45g) alfalfa sprouts

➤ Split the bread lengthwise, leaving a "hinge."
Spread the cut sides with 2 tablespoons of dressing.

➤ Arrange tomato, avocado, and cucumber slices
in the bread and top with alfalfa sprouts. Drizzle with
more dressing, as desired, then close the bread. Cut
across in portions and serve.

MIXED LEAF
& PEAR SALAD

MIXED LEAF & PEAR SALAD

SERVES 4

3 ounces (90g) mixed salad greens, such as red leaf
lettuce, frisée, or mâche (about 3 cups)
3 cups (125g) fresh young spinach leaves, washed
1 cup (30g) trimmed watercress
6 Belgian endive leaves, sliced
a few sprigs of chervil
2 tablespoons coarsely torn fresh tarragon
or basil
2 tablespoons chopped fresh chives
2 tablespoons chopped fresh flatleaf parsley
2 ripe but firm pears, cored and thinly sliced
½ cup (60g) toasted slivered almonds
Lemon Dressing (page 75)

➤ If the salad greens are large, tear them in smaller
pieces. Combine with the spinach leaves, watercress,
Belgian endive, all of the herbs, slices of pear, and
toasted almonds in a large serving bowl. Toss very
gently together, preferably using your hands.

➤ Prepare the lemon dressing, using either olive
or canola oil. Pour over the salad and toss lightly to
coat the ingredients. Serve at once.

SPICY
PEANUT DIP

SPLIT PEA SOUP

Deep green dried split peas are more flavorsome than the golden yellow kind, but both are suitable for making warming robust soups or purées.

SERVES 4

½ cup (100g) green or yellow split peas
2 teaspoons olive or canola oil
1 medium onion, chopped (about 1 cup [125g])
2 cloves garlic, minced
1 large carrot, sliced (about 1 cup [125g])
1 celery stalk, sliced (about ½ cup [60g])
1 medium potato, diced (about 1 cup [125g])
4 cups (1l) Fresh Vegetable Broth (page 75)
½ teaspoon ground allspice (*optional*)
2 tablespoons chopped cilantro
1 bay leaf
salt and freshly ground black pepper

～ Put the green or yellow split peas in a pan, cover with plenty of cold water, and bring to a boil. Boil rapidly for 10 minutes.

～ Meanwhile, heat the oil in a nonstick skillet and sauté the onion, garlic, carrot, and celery over medium heat until all the vegetables are soft and golden, about 10 minutes.

～ Drain the split peas and return to the rinsed pan. Add the softened vegetables, the potato, and broth. Stir in the allspice if using, cilantro, and bay leaf. Bring to a boil, then reduce the heat, cover, and simmer gently until the peas and vegetables are cooked, about 40 minutes.

～ Remove the bay leaf, and purée the soup in a blender or food processor. Return to the pan and reheat gently. Season to taste and serve very hot.

SPICY PEANUT DIP

Accompany this dip with a generous selection of freshly prepared raw vegetables, such as baby carrots, celery sticks, cucumber slices, snow peas, strips of red and green bell pepper, and some good bread.

SERVES 4

2 teaspoons olive or canola oil
1 small onion, minced (about ½ cup [60g])
2 garlic cloves, minced
¼ teaspoon chili powder
1 teaspoon ground cumin
1 teaspoon ground coriander
½ cup (125g) chunky natural peanut butter
(salt- and sugar-free)
¾ cup (180ml) water
2–3 teaspoons lemon juice
2–3 teaspoons tamari
raw vegetables for serving

～ Heat the oil in a small pan, add the onion, and sauté until soft and translucent. Add the garlic and spices and fry gently for 2–3 minutes, stirring.

～ Add the peanut butter to the pan and gradually stir in the water. Cook over low heat until thick. Remove from the heat and add lemon juice and tamari to taste. Let cool completely. Stir again to mix before serving with raw vegetables and bread.

CARROT & ORANGE SOUP

SERVES 4

2 teaspoons olive oil
1 small onion, minced (about ½ cup [60g])
a 1-inch (2.5-cm) piece of fresh ginger,
peeled and minced (*optional*)
1 garlic clove, minced
½ teaspoon ground coriander
½ teaspoon ground cumin
½ teaspoon chili powder
¼ teaspoon turmeric
1¼ pounds (600g) carrots, thinly sliced
(about 5 large carrots)
grated zest and juice of 1 large orange
1 large orange, peeled and chopped
3 cups (750ml) Fresh Vegetable Broth (page 75)
1–2 teaspoons fresh lemon juice
salt and freshly ground black pepper
cilantro leaves or twists of orange zest
for garnish (*optional*)

❧ Heat the oil in a saucepan, add the onion, ginger if using, garlic, and spices, and sauté gently for 3–5 minutes. Add the carrots and cook 8 minutes more, stirring frequently.

❧ Add the orange zest, chopped orange flesh, and broth to the pan. Bring to a boil, then reduce the heat, cover, and simmer gently about 20 minutes.

❧ Purée the soup in a blender or food processor. Reheat gently, then stir in the orange and lemon juices and season lightly or to taste.

❧ Serve garnished with cilantro leaves or twists of orange zest, if desired.

EGGPLANT & SESAME PÂTÉ

SERVES 4

2 medium eggplants (about ½ pound [250g] each)
1 garlic clove, minced
3 tablespoons light sesame paste (tahini)
2 tablespoons minced fresh mint or parsley
3 tablespoons low-fat plain yogurt
1–2 tablespoons lemon juice
salt and freshly ground black pepper
lemon wedges, raw vegetables, & breads for serving

❧ Preheat the oven to 350°F (180°C).

❧ Remove the eggplant stems, and prick the skin all over with a fork. Place the eggplants in a baking dish and bake in the preheated oven until they feel soft, 25–30 minutes. Let cool.

❧ Peel off the skin and chop the eggplant flesh. Purée in a blender or food processor with the garlic, tahini, mint or parsley, and yogurt. Add lemon juice, salt, and pepper to taste.

❧ Serve with the accompaniments suggested above.

CARROT & ORANGE SOUP

HEALTHFUL HEARTY FARE

Hearty meals need food that soothes, in preparation for pleasurable activity at the end of the day. Complex carbohydrates like pasta, rice, and potatoes, together with starchy, leafy, and green vegetables are the ideal. Add flesh foods if you must have them.

RIBBON VEGETABLES & SPAGHETTI

SERVES 4

2 medium carrots (about ¼ pound [125g])
1 medium zucchini (about ½ pound [250g])
½ medium leek
1 yellow bell pepper, seeded and thinly sliced
½ pound (250g) spaghetti
2 tablespoons olive oil
2 tablespoons fresh lime juice
2 tablespoons chopped fresh tarragon
salt and freshly ground black pepper
fresh tarragon leaves for garnish

RIBBON VEGETABLES
& SPAGHETTI

◦ Cut the carrots and zucchini into long, thin ribbons by drawing a swivel-bladed vegetable peeler down their length. Cut the leek into long, thin strips.

◦ Bring two large saucepans of water to a boil, then reduce the heat. Put all the vegetables in a steamer basket. Set the basket over one of the pans and cover. Cook until the vegetables are crisp-tender, 5–7 minutes. Meanwhile, cook the spaghetti in the other saucepan of boiling water until *al dente*.

◦ Combine the oil, lime juice, and tarragon in a small bowl and stir to mix.

◦ Drain the spaghetti and put into a warmed bowl with the vegetables. Add the dressing, season to taste and toss together. Garnish with fresh tarragon leaves.

Fresh Tomato & Basil Variation

Omit the lime juice and use fresh basil, oregano, chervil, or parsley instead of the tarragon. Add 2 large tomatoes, cubed, to the steamed vegetables and spaghetti. Dress with the olive oil.

SPINACH LASAGNA

SERVES 4

2 teaspoons olive or canola oil
1 medium onion, chopped (about 1 cup [125g])
1 garlic clove, minced
1 pound (500g) mushrooms, sliced
a few sprigs of fresh rosemary, roughly chopped
½ pound (250g) fresh spinach leaves, washed
½ pound (250g) lasagna (about 12 strips)
4 cups (900ml) Fresh Tomato Sauce (page 75)
1 cup (150g) shredded low-fat mozzarella cheese
1 cup (250ml) part-skim ricotta cheese
1 large egg
2 tablespoons pine nuts (*optional*)
3 tablespoons freshly grated Parmesan cheese

∾ Preheat the oven to 350°F (180°C).

∾ Heat the oil in a skillet and sauté the onion and garlic until soft and translucent, about 5 minutes. Add the mushrooms and rosemary and cook 8–10 minutes more, stirring frequently.

∾ Put the spinach in a saucepan with just the water that clings to the leaves after washing. Cook over medium heat until wilted and tender, about 7–10 minutes. Drain well and chop coarsely.

∾ Meanwhile, cook the lasagna strips, a few at a time, in a large saucepan of boiling water until almost *al dente*. Drain and rinse with cold water. Spread out the strips on a damp dish towel.

∾ Lightly grease a lasagna pan or other baking dish about 13 x 8 x 2 inches (32 x 23 x 5 cm). Spread 1 cup (250ml) of tomato sauce over the bottom. Cover with a third of the lasagna. Layer as follows: half the remaining tomato sauce, the mushrooms, another layer of lasagna, the remaining tomato sauce, the spinach, and mozzarella. Top with remaining lasagna.

∾ Lightly beat the ricotta cheese with the egg. Spread this mixture over the lasagna. Sprinkle with the pine nuts, if using, and the Parmesan.

∾ Bake in the preheated oven until golden brown and bubbling, 40–50 minutes.

MUSHROOM-STUFFED PASTA SHELLS

SERVES 4

2 teaspoons olive or canola oil
1 small onion, minced (½ cup [60g])
1 garlic clove, minced
1¼ pounds (600g) mushrooms, chopped
2 tablespoons chopped fresh rosemary
1 tablespoon chopped fresh parsley
1 cup (125g) crumbled feta cheese
½ cup (60g) pine nuts
¼ cup (45g) raisins
salt and freshly ground black pepper
20 jumbo pasta shells
4 cups (900ml) Fresh Tomato Sauce (page 75)
about ¾ cup (180ml) Fresh Vegetable
Broth (page 75)
chopped parsley for garnish

∾ Preheat the oven to 350°F (180°C).

∾ Heat the oil in a nonstick skillet, add the onion, and sauté 2–3 minutes. Add the garlic and the mushrooms and sauté a few minutes more, stirring from time to time. Stir in the rosemary and parsley and continue to cook until the liquid from the mushrooms has evaporated. Remove from the heat. Stir in half the cheese, the pine nuts, and raisins, and season lightly. Let cool.

∾ Cook the pasta shells in a large saucepan of boiling water until barely *al dente*. Drain well and spread out on paper towels to dry before filling.

∾ Purée the tomato sauce in a food processor or blender, gradually adding enough of the vegetable broth to make a smooth sauce with a thick, coating consistency.

∾ Fill the pasta shells with the mushroom mixture. Arrange the filled shells in a large baking dish, pour the tomato sauce over and around them, and then sprinkle with the remaining cheese. Cover the dish with foil and bake in the preheated oven for about 30–40 minutes.

∾ Sprinkle with chopped parsley, and serve with Mixed Leaf & Pear Salad (page 65).

VEGETABLE
RISOTTO

PASTA WITH TOMATOES & CHEESE

SERVES 4

4 large beefsteak tomatoes, cubed
¾ cup (180g) low-fat cottage cheese
¼ cup (7g) chopped fresh basil
1 large garlic clove, minced
2 tablespoons olive oil
salt and freshly ground black pepper
1 pound (500g) pasta, such as penne or fusilli
freshly grated Romano cheese for garnish (*optional*)

❧ Combine the tomatoes, cottage cheese, basil,
garlic, oil, and salt and pepper to taste in a bowl.
Mix gently together. If time allows, let stand for
about 2 hours so the flavors can blend.

❧ Cook the pasta in a large saucepan of boiling
water until *al dente*.

❧ Drain the pasta and return it to the saucepan.
Add the tomato mixture and fold together gently,
then warm over a low heat for a minute or two.

❧ Taste, and adjust the seasoning, and spoon onto
warmed plates. Sprinkle with the Romano cheese, if
using, and serve immediately.

VEGETABLE RISOTTO

SERVES 4

2 cups (175g) trimmed extra-fine asparagus tips
1 tablespoon olive or canola oil
2 shallots, chopped (about ¼ cup [30g])
1 garlic clove, minced
1½ cups (300g) short-grain or Arborio rice
Fresh Vegetable Broth (page 75)
a pinch of saffron threads (*optional*)
a strip of lemon peel
1 tablespoon lemon juice
2 cups (180g) sliced button mushrooms
8 sundried tomatoes packed in oil,
well drained and chopped
½ cup (60g) chopped walnuts or cashew nuts, toasted
salt and freshly ground black pepper
roughly chopped flatleaf parsley and large shavings of
Parmesan cheese (*optional*) for garnish

❧ Put the asparagus in a small saucepan of boiling
water and cook until barely tender, 2–3 minutes.
Drain, reserving the cooking liquid. Refresh the
asparagus in ice water and set aside.

❧ Heat the oil in a heavy saucepan. Add the
shallots and garlic and sauté 2–3 minutes. Stir in the
rice and cook 3 minutes, stirring occasionally.

❧ Add enough vegetable broth to the reserved
asparagus cooking liquid to make 3 cups (750ml).
Add to the pan with the saffron threads, if using,
and lemon peel and juice. Bring to a boil, then
reduce the heat, cover, and simmer 10 minutes.

❧ Add the mushrooms and sundried tomatoes and
cook, covered, until the rice is tender – another 10
minutes. Stir in the asparagus and nuts for the last
few minutes of cooking.

❧ Remove the lemon peel, season to taste, and
transfer to a warm dish. Sprinkle with chopped
parsley and large shavings of Parmesan cheese, if
using. Serve the risotto at once.

OVEN-BAKED VEGETABLES

SERVES 4

1 medium eggplant (about ¾ pound [350g])
1 fennel bulb (about ½ pound [250g]) *or* equivalent
quantity of small new potatoes, halved
1 medium onion
1 medium red bell pepper, seeded
1 medium yellow bell pepper, seeded
2 garlic cloves, minced
2 sprigs of fresh rosemary
2 sprigs of fresh thyme
2 bay leaves
4 teaspoons olive oil
1 medium zucchini (about ½ pound [250g])
½ pound (250g) cherry tomatoes
½ pound (250g) green beans (*optional*)
2 tablespoons balsamic vinegar
fresh basil leaves for garnish

~ Preheat the oven to 450°F (230°C). Cut the
eggplant in 1-inch (2.5-cm) cubes. Cut the fennel
and onion from top to bottom in 8 sections. Cut the
bell peppers in 1-inch (2.5-cm) cubes.

~ Arrange the eggplant, fennel or new potatoes,
onion, and bell peppers in an oiled nonstick roasting
pan. Add the garlic and herbs to the vegetables. Brush
with 3 teaspoons of the oil. Roast 20 minutes.

~ Meanwhile, slice the zucchini. Cut a small
cross in the top of each tomato. Remove the
vegetables from the oven, gently turn them
over, and add the zucchini, tomatoes, and
green beans if using. Brush the vegetables
with the remaining 1 teaspoon oil. Return
to the oven. Roast until all the vegetables
are tender, about 15 minutes longer.

~ Transfer to a warm dish, sprinkle with
the balsamic vinegar and basil, and serve.

PASTA WITH BUCKWHEAT

SERVES 4

2 cups (350g) kasha (roasted buckwheat groats)
4 cups (250g) farfalle (medium pasta butterflies)
or bowtie noodles
2 teaspoons unsalted butter
2 medium onions, minced (about 2 cups [250g])

~ Bring 4 cups (1l) of water to a boil in a small
saucepan. Add the kasha and then return to a boil.
Reduce the heat, cover, and simmer gently until
tender, 10–15 minutes.

~ Meanwhile, bring a large saucepan of water to a
boil, add the pasta, and cook until *al dente*.

~ Melt the butter in a small skillet, add the onion,
and sauté, stirring, until lightly browned.

~ Add the onion to the cooked kasha. Drain the
pasta and lightly toss with the kasha and onion
mixture. Serve at once. (Note *To serve four people as
a side dish, halve all the quantities.*)

OVEN-BAKED
VEGETABLES

BEAN CURD WITH VEGETABLES

SERVES 4

¾ pound (350g) firm tofu
4 tablespoons tamari
2 teaspoons sesame oil
2 garlic cloves, minced
1 tablespoon canola oil
3 scallions, trimmed and sliced
1 cup (125g) thinly sliced carrot
1 large yellow bell pepper, seeded and thinly sliced
1 cup (125g) snow peas, sliced lengthwise
1 cup (90g) sliced button mushrooms
1 cup (60g) bean sprouts
1 large beefsteak tomato (about ½ pound [250g]),
seeded and thinly sliced
1–2 tablespoons dry white wine or water
1 tablespoon sesame seeds (*optional*)

~ Drain the tofu, rinse well in running cold water, and dry on paper towels. Cut in ½-inch (1-cm) cubes using a serrated knife, and place in a shallow pan. Mix 2 tablespoons of the tamari with the sesame oil and half the garlic. Pour the mixture over the tofu and let marinate 1 hour, turning occasionally.

~ Preheat the broiler.

~ Set the pan of marinated tofu under the broiler and cook, turning from time to time, until crisp on all sides, 3–4 minutes.

~ Meanwhile, heat the canola oil in a large wok or skillet until very hot, add the scallions, carrot, bell pepper, and the remainder of the garlic, and stir-fry 2–3 minutes. Add the snow peas, mushrooms, and bean sprouts, and then the tomato. Stir-fry 2 minutes more. Finally, add the broiled marinated tofu, and stir-fry for a final minute.

~ In a bowl mix together the wine or water, and remaining tamari. Pour the mixture over the bean curd and vegetables. Toss briefly to mix.

~ Spoon into a hot serving dish, sprinkle with the sesame seeds if using, and serve immediately.

CHICKEN WITH ASPARAGUS

SERVES 4

4 teaspoons canola oil
1 medium onion, chopped (about 1 cup [125g])
1 garlic clove, minced
1 cup (90g) sliced mushrooms
1 pound (500g) skinless, boneless chicken cut
into 2-inch (5-cm) chunks
¾ cup (180ml) Fresh Vegetable Broth (page 75)
finely grated zest and juice of 1 small lemon
1 tablespoon capers, drained
2½ cups (300g) asparagus tips
2 tablespoons chopped fresh parsley
salt and freshly ground black pepper
fresh parsley leaves for garnish

~ Heat half the oil in a large nonstick skillet and gently sauté the onion and garlic for 3 minutes. Add the mushrooms and sauté 3 minutes more. Remove the vegetables with a slotted spoon and set them aside.

~ Heat the remaining oil in the pan and sauté the chicken slices until lightly browned all over, about 3 minutes.

~ Return the vegetables to the pan. Add the broth, lemon zest and juice, and capers and stir to mix. Bring to a boil, then reduce the heat. Cover and simmer for 5 minutes. Add the asparagus tips, and cook for 5 minutes more. Add the chopped parsley, stir to mix, and cook until the chicken is tender, about 5 minutes. Remove from the heat.

~ Season lightly or to taste, and serve garnished with fresh parsley leaves.

Bell Pepper & Butternut Squash Variation

Replace the mushrooms with 1 small, seeded and sliced green bell pepper. Replace the asparagus with an equivalent amount (or weight) of butternut squash, pumpkin, or yellow zucchini. Add both these vegetables to the pan after cooking the onion and proceed as for the remainder of the recipe. Omit the capers and use fresh tarragon in place of parsley.

MIXED SEAFOOD STEW

SERVES 4

1 pound (500g) skinless, boneless white fish,
such as striped bass
12 large raw shrimp
12 fresh mussels or small hardshell clams
4 cups (900ml) Fresh Tomato Sauce (page 75)
1 large green bell pepper, seeded and diced
a pinch of saffron threads
1 bay leaf
salt and freshly ground black pepper
chopped fresh parsley and grated lemon zest
for garnish

~ Cut the fish in 1½-inch (4-cm) cubes. Peel and devein the shrimp. Well scrub the mussels or clams. Set all the seafood aside.

~ Put the tomato sauce in a large saucepan, add the bell pepper, saffron threads, and bay leaf, and bring to a boil. Reduce the heat, cover, and simmer 5 minutes.

~ Add the cubes of fish and the mussels or clams to the sauce. Cover closely and cook 4-5 minutes (discard any mussels or clams that are still closed). Add the shrimp, pushing them down into the liquid, and cook until the shrimp have turned pink, 1–2 minutes longer.

~ Remove the bay leaf, and season to taste. Ladle the stew into wide, shallow bowls, and sprinkle with chopped parsley and grated lemon zest.

SALMON BAKED IN PARCHMENT

SERVES 4

olive or canola oil
4 salmon steaks (about 6 ounces [175g] each)
salt and freshly ground black pepper
4 sprigs of fresh dill, chopped
juice of 2 limes or small lemons
lime or lemon wedges for serving

~ Preheat the oven to 400°F (200°C). Cut out four parchment paper rectangles, each 12 x 8 inches (30 x 20 cm). Lightly brush with olive or canola oil.

~ Place a salmon steak on one half of each paper rectangle. Season lightly. Scatter chopped dill over each steak and sprinkle with lime or lemon juice.

~ Fold the paper over the salmon to enclose it, and roll and fold the edges firmly together to seal. Place the packages on a baking sheet and bake in the preheated oven until the salmon is just cooked and the packages are puffed up, 12–15 minutes.

~ Transfer the salmon steaks in their packages to four warmed plates. Serve immediately, with lime or lemon wedges to squeeze over each serving.

SIDE DISHES & BASIC RECIPES

These side dishes add valuable nutrients to hearty fare. Dressings bring zest to salads, moistness and bite to sandwiches. Both sauce and broth emphasize fresh vegetables and herbs, which lend a natural touch to baked pasta dishes, soups, and stews.

SPICY
COUSCOUS

SPICY COUSCOUS

Whole spices scent and flavor this aromatic side dish. Take care to remove the cinnamon stick and bay leaves before serving to family or guests.

SERVES 4

1 teaspoon cumin seeds
4 whole cloves (*optional*)
2 cups (500ml) hot Fresh Vegetable Broth (page 75)
6 cardamom pods, lightly crushed
½ cinnamon stick, lightly bruised
2 bay leaves
1½ cups (300g) couscous
salt and freshly ground black pepper
2 tablespoons pine nuts, toasted

⌒ Lightly toast the cumin seeds and cloves, if using, in a dry saucepan for 1–2 minutes. Remove from the heat, let cool slightly, then gradually add the broth. Add the cardamom pods, cinnamon stick, and bay leaves to the pan. Stir well, bring to a boil, and simmer 2 minutes.

⌒ Remove the pan from the heat and add the couscous. Stir well, then cover the pan and leave until the broth has been absorbed, about 5 minutes.

⌒ Remove the cinnamon stick and bay leaves. Season lightly or to taste. Serve hot, sprinkled with toasted pine nuts. (Note *Wash the cinnamon stick and use for garnish, if desired.*)

POTATOES WITH SPINACH

SERVES 4

3 potatoes (about 1 pound [500g]), peeled and diced
¾ pound (375g) fresh spinach leaves, washed
⅓ cup (90ml) milk
salt and freshly ground black pepper
a little grated nutmeg (*optional*)
4 egg whites

⌒ Preheat the oven to 400°F (200°C). Cook the potatoes and spinach in separate pans until tender. Drain the spinach, pressing out all water, and chop or purée. Drain and mash the potatoes with the milk. Add the spinach and seasoning to the potatoes.

⌒ Beat the egg whites until stiff, and fold gently into the mixture. Spoon into a lightly greased baking dish. Bake in the preheated oven until golden brown and puffed up, about 20–25 minutes. Serve at once.

LEMON DRESSING

2 tablespoons freshly squeezed lemon juice
3 tablespoons olive or canola oil
salt and freshly ground black pepper

∾ Combine all the ingredients in a bowl and mix with a fork until blended. Mix again before serving.

MUSTARD & HONEY DRESSING

2 tablespoons Dijon mustard
1 tablespoon honey
2 teaspoons lemon juice

∾ Combine all the ingredients in a bowl and mix with a fork until blended. Mix again before serving.

FRESH TOMATO SAUCE

MAKES 4 CUPS (900ML)

2 teaspoons olive or canola oil
1 small onion, chopped (about ½ cup [60g])
1 garlic clove, chopped
2 pounds (900g) ripe tomatoes, chopped
2 tablespoons chopped mixed fresh herbs, such as
basil, oregano, chervil, and parsley
salt and freshly ground black pepper

∾ Heat the oil in a large saucepan and add the onion and garlic. Cover the pan and let cook gently until softened, about 5 minutes.

∾ Add the tomatoes and the herbs. Cover again and cook gently until the tomatoes are broken down and saucelike, about 20 minutes. Stir occasionally.

∾ Season to taste. For a smooth sauce, purée in a blender or food processor. Make this sauce fresh, as required. (Note *If you cannot obtain good fresh tomatoes, substitute the same weight of canned peeled tomatoes. Before using, drain, then soak in the juice of 1 orange for an hour to give them a garden-fresh flavor.*)

FRESH VEGETABLE BROTH

MAKES ABOUT 5 CUPS (1.1L)

2 large carrots, sliced
1 large onion, sliced
2 outer celery stalks, sliced
a few celery leaves
a few parsley stems
2 sprigs each of fresh thyme and marjoram
2 bay leaves
3 garlic cloves, crushed with the side of a knife
a strip of lemon peel
10 black peppercorns
6 cups (1.3l) water

∾ Put all the ingredients in a large saucepan. Bring to a boil, then reduce the heat, cover the pan, and simmer until the vegetables are just soft but not mushy, about 45 minutes. Let cool.

∾ Strain the broth through a sieve into a large container, pressing the solids to extract as much liquid as possible. Keep covered in the refrigerator. Use the broth within 4 days.

FRESH
VEGETABLE
BROTH

75

WELLNESS INSURANCE

Vitamins, minerals, and herbs are some of nature's best catalysts to ensure energy balance. These nutrients are necessary to build and repair the body – including blood, bones, organs, and cells. Thus, complementing good nutrition with an appropriate formula of vitamins, minerals, and herbs can be regarded as wellness insurance. Be aware, however, that a poor diet supplemented with the most comprehensive formula will still be a poor diet.

FOR MOST people, supplements are a useful adjunct to healthful eating and exercise. They promote optimal balance, and help prevent the untimely appearance of chronic disease and avoidable illness.

While research data continually presents us with fresh information about nutritional supplements, the facts are often confusing. It is hard to keep up with every development and predict which claims will stand the test of time.

SUPPLEMENTS ARE ESSENTIAL

The serious diseases that were once common and dreaded hallmarks of dietary vitamin deficiency – scurvy (vitamin C), rickets (vitamin D), beri-beri (thiamin), and pellegra (niacin) – have now disappeared in all but the most deprived regions of the world. Nutritional supplements are used today primarily to protect against birth defects, heart disease, cancer, premature aging, infectious disease, cataracts, and strokes.

Medications, detrimental habits, and emotional stress drain essential nutrients from the body. Moreover, refining, processing, overcooking, and altering the genetic structure of food adversely affects its nutritional value. All these are facts of modern life that affect the assimilation and availability of nutrients from food. Wellness insurance is thus vital to ensure health and prevent disease.

SPECIAL CIRCUMSTANCES

People in particular age groups and circumstances will benefit from the health insurance of supplements.

Infants, children, and the elderly have unique needs that may not be fulfilled even with careful nutrition. Women who might conceive need folic acid – it is proven to prevent spina bifida and neural tube defects in the fetus. Active alcoholics and smokers need more vitamin C, folic acid, and zinc. Sexually active men need more zinc.

Maintaining good health is vital, whatever your chosen lifestyle and environment. You can insure it by taking a comprehensive formula similar to that shown on page 79.

NUTRITIONAL SUPPLEMENTS FOR OPTIMAL HEALTH

ANTIOXIDANTS & FREE RADICALS
Antioxidants are a powerful natural weapon to reverse the damage caused in the body by free radicals. This has led them to be called the fountain of youth – see p.77.

VITAMINS, MINERALS, & SUPPLEMENTS
Nutritional supplements are beneficial. They significantly enhance and improve a diet that emphasizes foods filled with the life-energy of the sun – see pp.78–79.

HERBS – NATURE'S OWN MEDICINE
Herbal remedies, which support your body's natural function and rebalance your energy, are often a gentler alternative to chemically synthesized drugs – see pp.80–81.

ANTIOXIDANTS & FREE RADICALS

FREE RADICALS are highly reactive, unstable molecules that are part of the body's natural aging process. They hunt for balanced molecules to bond with by stealing electrons from them in the process called oxidation, which leaves them unstable in return. Free radicals are increased by cigarette smoke, unhealthy food, and pollution. Antioxidants inhibit renegade free radicals and retard the damage they cause. No wonder they have been referred to as the *fountain of youth*.

SPINACH

TOMATOES

CURLY KALE

KIWI FRUIT   MANGO   PARSLEY

△ BETA CAROTENE
Converted into vitamin A in the body, beta carotene is a potent antioxidant and helps in the body's defense against free radical activity. It may also help prevent cataracts, the effects of aging, stroke, heart disease, and cancer.

△ VITAMIN C
This vitamin plays a vital role, building healthy bones and teeth, enabling the body to absorb iron, and helping it resist infection. Vitamin C appears to possess a remarkable ability to reduce the havoc caused by the electron-stealing molecules that accelerate aging, compromise healing, lessen immunity, and cause cancer.

AVOCADO

MUSSELS

SCALLOP

SOURDOUGH BREAD

ALMONDS

WHEAT GERM   PEANUTS

BRAZIL NUTS

△ VITAMIN E
Strong evidence suggests that vitamin E combats the degenerative process of premature aging by reducing oxidation. It also assists in preventing coronary heart disease, cataracts, and cancer. A diet that includes abundant amounts of leafy green vegetables, as well as nuts, vegetable oils, and wheat germ, will be rich in vitamin E.

△ SELENIUM
This essential trace element is a highly effective antioxidant and actually protects other antioxidants like vitamin E, vitamin C, and beta carotene while working with them to combat harmful oxidation of cell membranes. It protects the body against certain toxic metals such as cadmium and may reduce the risk of cancer.

VITAMINS, MINERALS, & SUPPLEMENTS

VITAMINS AND MINERALS are vital for almost every function in your body. Without them, you could not see, think, move, or breathe. Their most valuable source is from a diet that is rich in fruits, vegetables, and whole grains. Yet less than ten percent of people consume even the minimal recommended intake of such foods: five or more servings of fruits and vegetables a day. This is the type of diet that greatly decreases the incidence of cancer of the lung, larynx, mouth, esophagus, stomach, ovary, colon, rectum, bladder, pancreas, cervix, and uterus. It also significantly reduces the risks of heart attacks and strokes in both men and women. Many studies have been conducted about the positive benefits of vitamins and minerals for the efficient functioning of the body, but there is still a great deal to learn. However, two findings consistently emerge – that *nutritional supplements are beneficial*; and that *a diet emphasizing foods with life-energy is absolutely crucial to maintaining health.*

◁ VITAMIN A
The body converts beta carotene into vitamin A. It is required for healthy mucous membranes, skin, bones, and teeth. Vitamin A also helps with general and night vision.

WATERCRESS

MELON

◁ VITAMIN C
Vitamin C promotes immunity to infectious diseases and encourages tissue repair. It enables the body to absorb iron and reduces the risks of cataracts and many cancers.

GREEN BELL PEPPER

▷ B GROUP VITAMINS
The B vitamins work together to support energy release, cell growth, reproductive function, and the nervous system.

▷ VITAMIN D
Vitamin D is obtained primarily from exposure to sunlight but also from food sources. It is required for the absorption of calcium and phosphorus from the intestines.

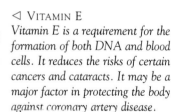

SARDINES

◁ NIACIN
Vitamin B$_3$ (Niacin) decreases elevated levels of blood cholesterol in the body. It is essential for the efficient metabolic breakdown of carbohydrates, fats, and proteins, and is required for the good health of the skin, nerves, and intestines.

◁ VITAMIN E
Vitamin E is a requirement for the formation of both DNA and blood cells. It reduces the risks of certain cancers and cataracts. It may be a major factor in protecting the body against coronary artery disease.

NUTS

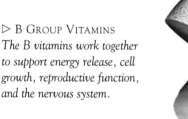

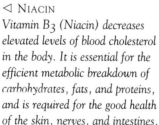

▷ FOLIC ACID
This B vitamin regulates cell division and is necessary for a healthy immune system. It protects against heart disease in adults and helps prevent neural tube defects (spina bifida) in the fetus.

ORANGE

WHOLE GRAINS

GREEN PEAS

▷ VITAMIN K
Vitamin K enables normal blood clotting. It prevents hemorrhage. It is also thought to help prevent certain types of cancer.

CABBAGE

FRESH DATES

◁ CALCIUM
This mineral is necessary for bone growth, blood coagulation, and the proper function of nerves and muscles. It helps lower blood fat, regulate blood pressure, and is essential for a healthy heart.

▷ SELENIUM
This mineral is required for a healthy immune system. It works with other antioxidants to protect against the damage of free radicals and oxidation.

ONIONS

RUBY GRAPEFRUIT

◁ MAGNESIUM
This mineral ensures the proper function of nerves and muscles. It supports the immune system and is a necessary catalyst for energy production.

▷ MANGANESE & CHROMIUM
Manganese is a mineral needed in the synthesis of thyroid hormone. Chromium is a mineral that helps with regulating the levels of blood sugar and cholesterol.

DRIED LEGUMES

WHOLE GRAIN BREAD

▷ ZINC
This mineral is required for proper healing and immunity. It is also vital for the formation of insulin and protein and is a catalyst for the synthesis of DNA.

"PHYSICIAN'S FORMULA" WELLNESS INSURANCE

⌒

This is an optimal daily formula for most adults. The ingredients and doses are based on the best available information. Remember that a poor diet with supplements will *still* be a poor diet. The best insurance for health is a variety of foods filled with life-energy, supported by the following nutrients.

Vitamin A (*as beta carotene*)	25,000	IU
Vitamin B_1	20	mg
Vitamin B_2	20	mg
Vitamin B_6	20	mg
Vitamin B_{12}	20	mcg
Niacin	20	mg
Biotin	100	mcg
Pantothenic Acid	30	mg
Folic Acid	400	mcg
Vitamin C	1000	mg
Vitamin D	400	IU
Vitamin E	400	IU
Vitamin K	100	mcg
Calcium	500	mg
Phosphorus	375	mg
Selenium	100	mcg
Magnesium	100	mg
Iron (*ferrous fumarate*)	18	mg
Copper	2	mg
Zinc	30	mg
Manganese	5	mg
Chromium	100	mcg

• Purchase a reputable brand for consistent and assured quality, purity, and freshness.
  • Make sure the supplements you choose are free of sugar, artificial colors, and preservatives.
  • Folic acid (400 mcg) is a vital supplement for all women who might become pregnant.
  • Women of child-bearing age may benefit from the supplement of iron suggested above. Men do not ordinarily require extra iron in their diet.

HERBS – NATURE'S OWN MEDICINE

HERBAL remedies were used with great success long before the chemically synthesized drugs of medicine today. Knowledge of herbs and cures was passed from one generation to the next in a tradition that survives in countries such as India and China, where healing is still concerned with balance and harmony of body, mind, and spirit. While science and technology have provided us with many valuable drugs, the gently therapeutic properties of nature's medicine remain available for many common ailments. So, next time sinus congestion, or headache, or indigestion has you running to the local pharmacy, consider a herbal remedy instead. Herbal remedies deserve a place in your home. These kinder alternatives support your body's natural function and rebalance your energy. Plant essences and aromas are also worth discovering. Inhaling the scent of *jasmine* or *rose* may evoke memories of the past, and may be all you need to transform fatigue into life-energy.

FRESH PLANT

FRESH FLOWER HEAD

FRESH LEAF

△ MILK THISTLE
(*Silybum marianum*)
The seeds are used to help regenerate liver function. They may also help to relieve gallstone colic. The leaves are used for indigestion and lack of appetite.

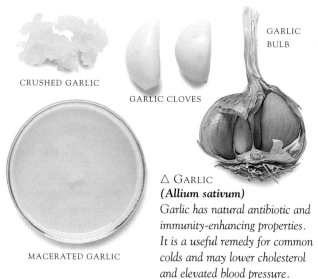

CRUSHED GARLIC

GARLIC CLOVES

GARLIC BULB

MACERATED GARLIC

△ GARLIC
(*Allium sativum*)
Garlic has natural antibiotic and immunity-enhancing properties. It is a useful remedy for common colds and may lower cholesterol and elevated blood pressure.

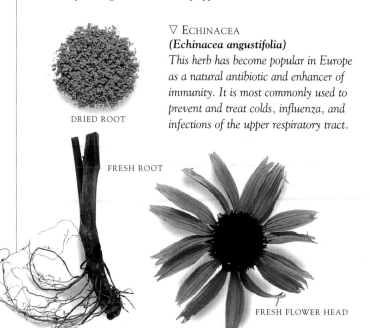

DRIED ROOT

FRESH ROOT

FRESH FLOWER HEAD

▽ ECHINACEA
(*Echinacea angustifolia*)
This herb has become popular in Europe as a natural antibiotic and enhancer of immunity. It is most commonly used to prevent and treat colds, influenza, and infections of the upper respiratory tract.

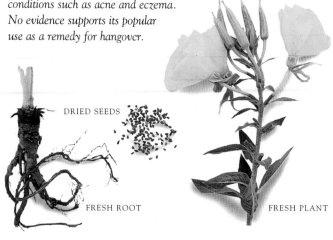

DRIED SEEDS

FRESH ROOT

FRESH PLANT

▽ EVENING PRIMROSE
(*Oenothera biennis*)
The seed oil has been demonstrated to be an effective treatment for premenstrual syndrome and also for a variety of skin conditions such as acne and eczema. No evidence supports its popular use as a remedy for hangover.

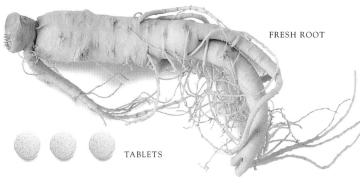

FRESH ROOT

TABLETS

CAPSULES

△ GINSENG
(Panax ginseng)
Ginseng is widely used to increase stamina, strengthen sexual desire, relieve stress, and resist illness. Research indicates that it may help lower cholesterol, regulate blood sugar, and protect the liver and heart besides.

DRIED SEEDS

DRIED LEAVES

FRESH LEAF

△ GINKGO
(Ginkgo biloba)
Ginkgo improves circulation, in particular blood flow to the brain. It is valued for treating memory loss and for relieving depression.

TINCTURE

▽ SCHIZANDRA
(Schisandra chinensis)
One of the most popular systemic tonics in China contains schizandra berries as an essential ingredient. The tonic is well known as an aphrodisiac. Schizandra is used to alleviate skin irritation and allergy and to treat insomnia

FRESH LEAFY STEM

DRIED FRUIT

SELF-HELP HERBAL REMEDIES TO TREAT COMMON AILMENTS

Many people in the world still regard herbs as the preferred choice for treating myriad common ailments and everyday problems. Indeed, the debt to plants as the original source of some of our most valuable modern medicines must be acknowledged. Quinine from cinchona, ephedrine from ma huang, morphine from opium poppy, and digitalis from foxglove are important examples.

Numerous gentle remedies that have truly stood the test of time are available and safe to use in the form of teas, tonics, capsules, inhalations, oils, and salves. The following remedies are intended just as a guide. Refer to a reputable herbal reference book to learn about properties, preparation, and dosage. If in doubt, consult a registered herbal practitioner.

Stress relief Chamomile, lavender, linden (lime), evening primrose, sage, skullcap, valerian.
Colds, coughs, & congestion Anise, cinnamon, elder, eucalyptus, garlic, ginger, pine, rosehip.
Sore throat Garlic, myrrh, rosemary, sage, thyme.
Indigestion Anise, chamomile, cinnamon, fennel, ginger, licorice, peppermint, slippery elm.
Diarrhea Comfrey, ginger, peppermint.
Constipation Aloe vera, dandelion, fenugreek, licorice, senna.
Nausea Basil, chamomile, ginger, peppermint.
Sleeplessness Chamomile, cowslip, lavender, nightcap, passionflower, valerian.
Headache & Migraine Chamomile, feverfew, wood betony.
Abrasions & Wounds Aloe vera, chamomile, marigold, plantain, shepherd's purse.
Fatigue, Gloom, & Despondency Angelica, anise, cardamom, cayenne, elder, fennel, feverfew, ginseng, lemon balm, sage, St. John's wort, vetiver, vervain.
Prostate Enlargement Damiana, ginseng, *Pygeum africanum*, saw palmetto.
Menstrual Difficulties Black cohosh, damiana, dong quai, goldenseal, licorice, marigold, milk thistle, red raspberry, sarsaparilla, red clover.
Urinary Tract Infections Cranberry, dandelion, licorice, parsley.

ENJOYABLE EXERCISE

Exercise is an absolute requirement for achieving balanced energy and health. The best kind of exercise is activity that makes you breathe faster, and smile as well. A sense of playfulness helps, and is beneficial. Even the smallest increase in physical activity will help to lower levels of stress and the risk of disease. Step Two identifies the second ideal – wellness walking and yoga.

ENJOYABLE EXERCISE
EINSTEIN ENERGY DIET

CAN YOU recall when you last ran down the street? When did you last laugh out loud at the joy of being alive or revel in your own stamina? Exercise does not have to be an intense workout that you approach with tremendous seriousness. The best exercise is activity that finds a place in your daily life, and that you find enjoyable and fun. Even moderate exercise can restore and maintain physical energy balance. It is most beneficial if done at least five days a week, for twenty minutes a day; or, if necessary, ten minutes twice a day. Regular small increases in physical activity – climbing stairs instead of taking an elevator – also contribute significantly to levels of wellness. Start by exercising as often as you can while still feeling good about it. You might want to remind yourself that jogging with your dog or raking leaves can be just as much exercise as working out in the gym or swimming.

Step Two of the Pyramid entails a combination of Wellness Walking (pages 96 and 97) and an easy yoga routine that anyone can do.

WALK YOUR WAY TO WELLNESS
For individuals of any age and fitness level, brisk walking with an energetic stride brings as many benefits as a high-intensity workout. Moreover, because some decline is a natural part of aging, exercise becomes increasingly beneficial as you get older. Try to get outside, get huffy and puffy – and just enjoy yourself. Nothing could be better for your body, mind, and spirit.

BENEFITS OF EXERCISE

Regular daily exercise has many benefits as well as the ability to balance your physical energy.

- It improves your circulation, lowers your blood pressure, and strengthens your heart.
- It tones muscles and helps you lose excess body fat.
- It strengthens and nourishes your immune system.
- It lessens the occurrence of headaches and backaches.
- It increases your stamina.
- It gives you more energy for satisfying and pleasurable sex.
- It maintains supple joints and strong bones.
- It increases concentration.
- It decreases levels of stress, worry, and anxiety.

INNER HARMONY & PEACE

Yoga stimulates your *healing force* and creates a pathway to virtually unlimited wellness. When practiced together with proper breathing and ethics, yoga postures strengthen, relax, and improve the flexibility of muscles and joints. They improve circulation to help prevent heart attacks. The program illustrated in the following pages is appropriate for any type of person, regardless of strength, flexibility, and age. The physical well-being, peace of mind, and inner calm that yoga induces are the truest sources of happiness and wellness. Yoga will help you enjoy lasting energy and vitality.

A DAILY YOGA ROUTINE

A regular time for your routine is preferable; just before your wellness walk, it will give you extra stamina. Find a convenient time, but wait at least an hour after eating before starting. Aim to spend twenty minutes on your daily routine. Practice outdoors whenever it is possible, surrounded by sunlight and fresh air. If indoors, then choose a space that

faces a window. Wear comfortable clothing so you can breathe and move unrestrained. Never speed through your yoga routine or push yourself too far or fast. Hurrying will only work against your goals, especially backache relief, weight loss, and stress management. The sequence of postures on pages 84

to 95 is designed to strengthen and stretch the whole body, to calm the mind, and support the spirit. As you become more comfortable with the yoga postures, you will hold them longer and naturally breathe better. Your yoga routine will become an everyday pleasure that is rich in its rewards of happiness and health.

YOU CAN DO IT
This yoga program is ideal for everyone. Levels of flexibility present no problem because both limber and stiff people can ease into the gentle postures. The more challenging postures are shown with a simple modification. Do not strain. Just listen to your body and breathe properly. Regular yoga practice balances energy and stimulates your healing force.

YOGA PRACTICE

The essence of daily yoga practice is the Sanskrit word, Namaste, I salute the divinity in you.

❧

- The ethos of yoga is harmony, deep relaxation, and peace.
- Establish a deep, calm, and even breathing rhythm.
- Focus your thoughts in one place. Find a spot in the middle distance and use it throughout the exercises.
- Before beginning your routine, find a restful and peaceful place to practice.
- As you come out of a posture, be sure to relax thoroughly before slowly standing up.
- For most poses, repeat the movement several times.

WELLNESS YOGA

Yoga is the harmonious balance of body, mind, and spirit. It helps restore the unity of your whole being. Wellness Yoga integrates yoga postures from ancient India with breathing practices and timeless ethics. Virtually every aspect of your health will be influenced by yoga practice. It has many physical benefits but most people experience a more profound effect: a sense of inner peace and calm that is the heart of wellness.

YOGA ethics honors the divinity in all life. It consists of timeless codes for living that harmonize your emotions, and cause you to reflect a sense of inner peace in what you think, say, and do. Practicing yoga actively encourages *positive feelings and attitudes*, especially an increased capacity to love and forgive. From this spring the qualities of kindness, honesty, and peacefulness that help you treat others as you would wish to be treated yourself. Living in the present, keeping your mind active, and being aware of community and environmental needs are also vital. Follow this *ninefold* code for a deep sense of purpose and infinite peace.

PRACTICE YOUR BREATHING

Breath is the ultimate source of vitality. Correct breathing during yoga exercise requires practice. To begin, inhale slowly and deeply, feeling your breath move steadily upwards to fill your abdomen, lower lungs, and then your upper lungs. Exhale slowly, and feel your breath descend in the opposite direction. To become used to breathing this way, rest your hands on your abdomen to feel its expansion and contraction, and the movement of your breath in and out. Practice as often as you can, during or between yoga postures as well as when you feel the need to relax and unwind.

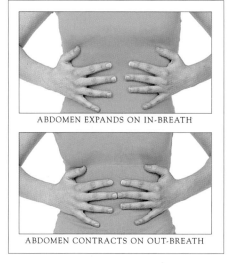

ABDOMEN EXPANDS ON IN-BREATH

ABDOMEN CONTRACTS ON OUT-BREATH

THE NINE ETHICS OF YOGA

Be Loving & Forgiving

Be Kind & Empathetic

Be Non-violent & Seek Peace

Be Honest with Perfect Integrity

Protect the Environment

Engage in Lifelong Learning

Contribute to the Community

Follow the Golden Rule

Stay in the Here & Now

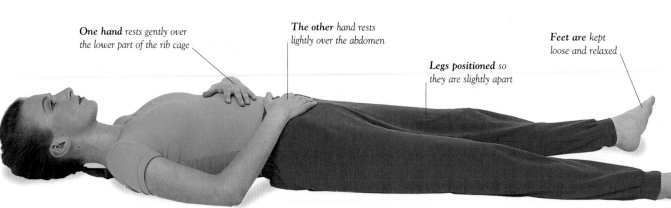

One hand *rests gently over the lower part of the rib cage*

The other *hand rests lightly over the abdomen*

Legs positioned *so they are slightly apart*

Feet are *kept loose and relaxed*

LEG STRETCHES

THESE EASY leg stretches encourage healthy circulation in your lower body and help to revitalize your hips, legs, and feet. By stretching and strengthening the leg muscles you keep your lower back limber and protect it from daily stress.

Exercises that build strength in the legs such as running, walking, or bicycling should be balanced with these yoga postures that improve flexibility. Strength and suppleness in the legs are necessary for a strong back which promotes correct posture.

Knees bent comfortably. Both feet are kept flat on the floor

Shoulders opened out and pressed lightly against the floor. Try to keep them relaxed

Hands clasped together around the shins for support

The neck is straight and relaxed, the eyes look forwards and upwards

The sole of the foot is flexed to increase the stretch down the back of the leg

Knees bent slightly to avoid any strain on muscles and tendons

Upper back and shoulders pressed firmly to the floor. Do not lift them off the floor

Knee bent at an acute angle but still feeling comfortable

Foot placed firmly on the floor beneath the knee

1 Lie on your back with knees bent and rest both feet flat on the floor, just beneath your knees. Stretch your arms out beside your body with palms facing upwards. Press your lower back firmly into the floor. Breathe deeply and relax.

2 Inhale deeply. Then as you exhale, use your stomach muscles to hug your knees close to your chest, clasping your hands around your lower legs for support only. As you begin to relax, allow your lower back to lift slightly off the floor.

3 Lower the left foot gently to the floor, bending the knee. Slowly extend the right foot towards the sky, stretching out the leg. If your muscles are tight, keep the right knee slightly bent to avoid any possible strain. Breathe into the stretch. Repeat the posture with the other leg.

RAG DOLL

THE SMOOTH, flowing motion of the Rag Doll allows the spine to lengthen while releasing physical and emotional tension from the neck, shoulders, back, and legs, where it tends to build up. The posture utilizes gravity to release blocked energy at the base of the spine and encourage its upward flow. Bending at the hips stimulates your circulation. This balances energy and invigorates your body, mind, and spirit. Be cautious if you are prone to either dizziness or high blood pressure.

Head held and kept centered between the shoulders, with chin parallel to the floor

Take deep, complete, and relaxed breaths throughout the whole sequence

Chin lowered gently to the chest. Do not strain or force chin into position

Bend forward softly from the waist. Stop at the point that feels most comfortable

1 Standing tall with good posture, inhale deeply and draw your hands into a prayer position in front. Do not lock your knees. Exhaling slowly, focus your eyes straight ahead.

2 Inhale and exhale deeply. Rest your arms by your sides and lower your chin to your chest. Begin to curl your upper body forward with your arms hanging loosely in front.

Knees slightly bent – not locked. No tension should be felt at either the back of the knees or the thighs

3 Without straining, bend forward as far as you can. Hold the posture for several minutes. Return to your original position, one vertebra at a time, keeping your chin tucked in. Close your eyes and feel how relaxed you have become.

Fingers rest on the floor. Just let them reach a level that is comfortable if this is not possible.

HALF MOON

THE HALF MOON creates balance, strength, and flexibility. Just as the moon directs the tides, so this posture gently harmonizes both sides of the body. As we age, the spine's flexibility tends to diminish. This posture awakens that flexibility, keeps the spine supple, and restores strength through the body. The stretching opens up the hips and ribcage, helping to increase circulation and the flow of breath.

Arms *raised up over the head, with elbows kept slightly bent*

After the stretch, *return to an upright position. As you exhale, lower your arms to your sides*

Abdominal and back muscles *both help support the stretch, and will gradually increase in strength and tone*

Knees *remain relaxed – not locked in position – during the whole sequence*

To help maintain balance *throughout this posture, keep your feet together, pressed flat and firm against the floor*

1 With feet together and weight over your arches, find your balance. Inhale, lift your arms above your head, resting your palms together. Now stretch your body tall and rise upwards.

2 As you exhale, bend your upper body to the right. Keeping your head relaxed, hold for at least three complete breaths. Inhale and slowly return to an upright position.

3 Repeat the posture again, extending your arms high above your head and gently bending your upper body to the left. As you hold the sideways stretch, roll your shoulders gently backwards so that your chest is opened and expands.

87

TREE

THE TREE pose is a balancing yoga posture. It requires concentration, but with practice, patience, and a simple modification (see below), anybody can achieve this posture and enjoy its benefits. The Tree will improve your balance and strengthen your legs. The balance you achieve in this posture will be reflected in your emotions, creating a feeling of unwavering centeredness and calm. These qualities will enhance the positive benefits of the rest of the yoga postures to follow.

Eyes focused on a fixed point at eye level, like a spot on the wall

Sole of foot flat against the thigh, as high above the knee as possible

1 Stand up tall and straight. Sway gently and find your center of balance. Focus your eyes on a point. Breathe slowly.

2 Put your weight on your left foot. Draw your right foot up to rest on your inner left thigh, then exhale slowly.

Palms joined together in the prayer position at chest level

3 Inhale and lift palms to a prayer position. Breathe calmly, holding the posture as long as it is comfortable. Lower your foot to the floor and stand upright. Feel calm. Repeat the whole sequence standing on your right foot.

MODIFIED POSITION

Stand a little way from the chair in a balanced position. Rest one hand securely on its back. Keep your hand on the chair for support as you follow steps 2 and 3.

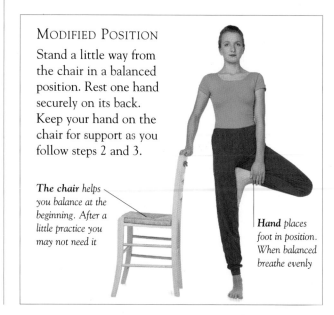

The chair helps you balance at the beginning. After a little practice you may not need it

Hand places foot in position. When balanced breathe evenly

Foot planted firmly on the floor. Toes spread out help with balance

TRIANGLE

THIS POSE helps build strength and suppleness throughout the entire body. It stretches and tones the muscles on the side of the body and improves the flexibility of the spine. The hips, legs, abdomen, and shoulders are also stretched out and strengthened. In this yoga posture, take care not to overextend or put undue tension on your knees. A good method to use when learning the triangle is to stand with your back against a wall and your feet a little way out from the wall.

Arms stretched out as long as possible, reaching out through the fingertips

1 Stand upright with feet apart. Inhale deeply, and lift your arms up to shoulder level with your palms facing down. Exhale, relax your shoulders, and stretch out.

Legs at least a shoulder-width apart and feet planted firmly on the floor

Hand reaching up towards the sky with fingers together and palm facing outwards

2 Inhale and turn your left foot out by ninety degrees. Exhale and bend your upper body to the left, with back flat. Reach your right hand up, your left hand down. Look upwards. Repeat on the other side.

Breathe slowly and deeply. Take three complete breaths while holding this position

Hand holding the ankle firmly for support

EXTENDED POSITION

After holding the posture shown in step 2, extend your right arm over your head and look straight ahead. Every time you inhale, reach through your fingers to extend your arm more fully. To come out of this pose, raise your arm to the sky, and stand upright.

Feet firmly on the floor and kept in the correct position throughout the exercise

Hand resting beside foot. If you are unable to reach the foot, rest your hand as far down the leg as possible

SITTING TAILOR

IT IS IMPORTANT to have an element of balance in your yoga routine, to combine the calming, relaxing poses with the more physically exertive and energizing postures. Relaxation poses such as this one comfort you and enable you to focus on the energy that is released throughout the body during yoga. It looks simple, but the Sitting Tailor brings its own challenges. Many of us have difficulty in sitting still and this pose helps to quiet the restless body and mind.

1 Sit with legs crossed. Lengthen your spine. Fold your fingers in front of you, inhale deeply, raise your arms above your head, palms up. Exhale, relax your shoulders.

Upper body stretched tall and straight, with the shoulders and neck released from tension

The stretch is felt in the neck and through the shoulders

Arms wrapped around shoulders, left elbow over right elbow

COMFORTING EMBRACE

After step 1, wrap your arms around your shoulders. Sit tall, breathe deeply, and tuck your chin in to your chest. Embrace yourself and feel the stretch.

2 Inhale deeply. Exhale and release all your fingers. Slowly lower your arms and fold your hands in your lap. Keeping your back straight, take a few slow, relaxing breaths. Feel your body released from physical tensions.

Sit still in a relaxed position with knees crossed. Use a soft cushion to sit on, if preferred

Hands folded loosely and placed comfortably in the lap

Feet beneath the knees in a relaxed posture

CHILD'S POSE

BRINGING relaxation to the whole body is an integral part of yoga. The Child's Pose is a gentle, inverted posture which encourages the flow of blood to your brain and refreshes and lightens your mind. The gentle pressure that is exerted on your thighs and calves squeezes excess fatigue from tired legs and stimulates circulation in the lower body. If this pose causes discomfort in your knees, try placing a pillow between your buttocks and legs for added support and relief.

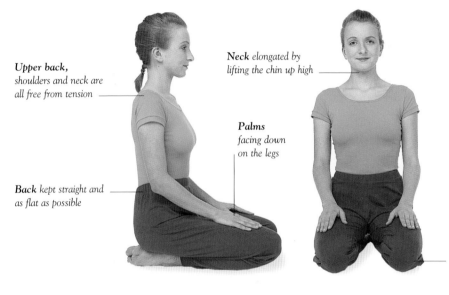

Upper back, shoulders and neck are all free from tension

Back kept straight and as flat as possible

Neck elongated by lifting the chin up high

Palms facing down on the legs

Knees slightly apart, resting lightly on the floor

1 Find a peaceful, quiet place and then sit in a kneeling position, resting on your heels. Move your buttocks comfortably onto the soles of your feet. Place your hands, palms facing down, on the front of your legs. Inhale deeply and stretch up tall and straight out of your hips, lifting up through your torso and chest. Exhale slowly and finally relax your shoulders and your neck.

Buttocks kept in position, resting lightly on the heels

Body bent forward with a flat, straight back

Hands relaxed by the side of the feet with palms facing upwards

2 Inhale, and as you exhale bend forward with a flat back, bringing your chest to your knees. Rest your forehead on the floor, arms by your sides, palms upwards. If it is more comfortable, stretch your arms out in front of you. Take a few deep, slow breaths.

91

CAT

THE BACKBONE of physical wellness is literally a strong and supple spine. The Cat posture both flexes and stretches your back muscles and elongates the spinal column. Alternately arching and curving your spine keeps it flexible and aids correct alignment. This pose relieves tension in your entire back, making it easier for energy to flow freely through the spine. The Cat is helpful for people who experience some discomfort in their lower back from long hours of sitting down.

Spine elongated *from the tailbone to the base of the head*

Head held *up straight and firm*

Hands pressed *into the floor with fingers straight out in front*

Back curled *and rounded upwards towards the sky*

Both elbows *are kept straight and firm, but not locked*

1 Kneel on the floor with your knees beneath your hips and your hands underneath your shoulders. Point your fingers straight ahead. Inhale deeply and then elongate your spine.

2 Exhale, and curl your back towards the sky. Tuck your chin to your chest and press your palms firmly into the floor. Take a slow, deep breath and feel the stretch for a few seconds.

3 Inhale, then raise your chin and lengthen your spine to create a small dip in your lower back. Pull your shoulders down from your ears, feeling the stretch in your upper back. Keep your elbows straight and your head relaxed. Take three complete breaths. Then repeat the sequence three more times.

Spine curved *with a small dip in the lower to middle part of the back*

Neck stretched *forward but not hyperextending*

Pelvis is tilted *slightly, which helps to support the muscles in the lower part of the back*

Feet are close, *with toes resting lightly on the floor*

Knees directly *beneath the hips are firmly supporting the posture*

COBRA

THE COBRA POSTURE creates a gentle backward bend that is vital to help maintain flexibility in the spine. It helps to increase suppleness and develops the muscles in your back and buttocks. It also increases your awareness of the energy in your spine and stimulates its positive upward flow towards your brain. Lifting the upper body away from the floor stretches your upper spine while building muscular strength in your lower back. It helps relieve tension throughout your whole back.

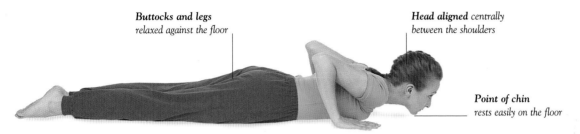

Buttocks and legs *relaxed against the floor*

Head aligned *centrally between the shoulders*

Point of chin *rests easily on the floor*

1 Lie on your front with your legs relaxed against the floor. Bend your elbows, keeping them close to your sides and rest your palms flat on the floor under your shoulders. Rest your chin on the floor.

Back muscles *used to raise the chest from the floor*

Hands *facing forward with palms pressed into the floor*

Head *raised up so that both eyes can gaze upwards and concentrate*

2 Inhaling slowly, raise your chin and chest off the floor, using only your back muscles to lift you. Keep your palms lightly on the floor. As you exhale, pull your shoulders away from your ears.

3 Inhale deeply. As you exhale, press with your arms to deepen the arch in your back. Keep your abdomen and hips on the floor. Exhaling, lower your body to the floor. Repeat three times.

Upper back *between the shoulders feels the stretch*

Back arched *only as far as it is comfortable*

Feet close *together with toes pointed*

LATERAL TWIST

THE SPINE HAS now been stretched forwards, backwards, and sideways. To complete the range of movements, practice this pose. Gentle spinal twists adjust the vertebrae and help keep the cushionlike disks between vertebrae supple.

This posture helps to keep the spine limber and makes the muscles that surround and support the spine stronger. The subtle pressure created in the digestive area helps digestion. It also opens up the chest and releases emotional tension.

Head upright and erect, stretching upwards to create a straight line from buttocks to the top of the head

Left leg outstretched in front and relaxed into the floor

Left arm raised skywards, keeping close to the side of the head

Right knee bent and crossed over left leg, level with the knee

Foot flexed with toes pointing up to the sky

1 Sit up with legs outstretched. Bend your right knee and cross it over your left leg, resting your right foot beside your left knee.

2 Place your right hand behind you for support. Stretch your left arm up to the sky. Inhale deeply and lengthen the spine.

Shoulders opened up as far as is comfortable to assist in relaxation

3 Exhale and twist your upper body to the right. Lower your left arm so that your elbow presses against the outside of your right knee. As you inhale, elongate your spine, twisting as you exhale. Hold for three slow breaths. Come out of the pose while exhaling. Now relax. Repeat with right arm upward and left leg bent.

Elbow placed in front of bent right knee

Right elbow pressed in close to the side of the body helps positioning and balance

Fingers spread out slightly help create a broader base of support

RELAX

THE BENEFITS OF YOGA are enhanced when you follow your routine with a period of peaceful relaxation. During this practice all of the energy that is released through yoga postures is drawn inwards, and it can help as much with flexibility, strength, and health as the more active poses do. Relaxation takes you into a deeper level of calm and peace instilled by yoga postures. When you sink fully into relaxation, your body, mind, and spirit feel thoroughly restored and regenerated.

TOTAL RELAXATION

Lie on your back and stretch out, using a blanket for warmth if you wish. Close your eyes. Let your arms relax at your sides, palms upwards. Relax your legs, slightly apart, and allow your feet to rest with toes pointing outwards. Mentally scan your body for any lingering tension. Now consciously let go of the tension as you exhale. Let your breathing flow rhythmically.

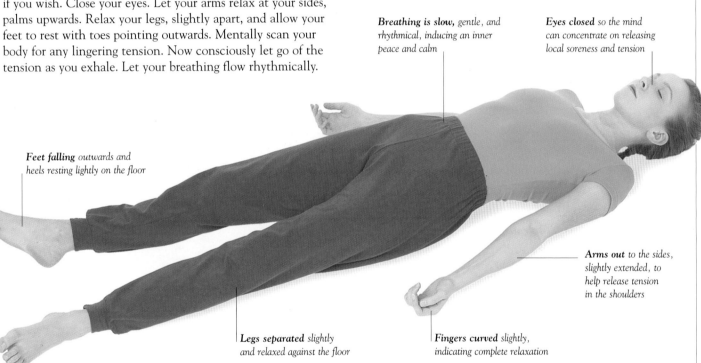

Breathing is slow, gentle, and rhythmical, inducing an inner peace and calm

Eyes closed so the mind can concentrate on releasing local soreness and tension

Feet falling outwards and heels resting lightly on the floor

Arms out to the sides, slightly extended, to help release tension in the shoulders

Legs separated slightly and relaxed against the floor

Fingers curved slightly, indicating complete relaxation

MODIFIED POSITION 1

Any soreness or tension you experience in your lower back can be relieved by simply bending your knees and resting your feet on the floor in front of you. Your back has more support now.

Neck stretched lightly releases tension in the upper part of the body

MODIFIED POSITION 2

For an especially sore or tense back, rest your legs up on a chair placed in front of you. This position enables your back to be fully supported and at the same time, free from any tension.

Awareness of the slow rhythm of your breathing enables you to relax

WELLNESS WALKING

*Wellness Walking is fast becoming the most popular way to encourage feelings of vibrant health.
You can "wellness walk" outdoors in the fresh air, or indoors on a track or in a shopping mall.
Wellness walking is good aerobic exercise. It stimulates
your body's cardiovascular system and raises your
levels of stamina, endurance, and joy in living.*

Shoulders *held straight and
encouraged to relax*

Abdomen muscles
*held firm, supporting
the muscles of the
lower back*

Back *straight and upright,
not arched back or bent over*

Comfortable, well-fitting
*shoes cushion feet and
avoid sore spots*

Heel naturally *strikes the ground
first, propelling the body forward
as the foot rolls from heel to toe*

IDEAL exercise consists of a balance
between moderate exertion, mental
concentration, and a sense of play.

A combination of the yoga routine
shown on pages 84 to 95 and wellness
walking is ideal exercise, giving you
all the benefits of an intense workout.
Walk for at least twenty minutes at a
comfortably brisk pace – but enough
to get out of breath – with arms and
legs swinging rhythmically in unison.
You will soon feel blood and energy
flowing to every part of your body.

• Pay attention to maintaining good
  posture throughout your walk.

• Breathe evenly and rhythmically at
  all times during your walk.

• Always wear comfortable shoes and
  loose-fitting, warm clothing.

• Swing your arms back and forward,
  raising the forearms so they are at
  right angles to the upper arms. Let
  your hands form loose fists. Keep
  your neck and shoulders relaxed.

• As your leg reaches forward, let the
  hips rotate downward and forward.
  This helps develop a gliding rhythm
  that feels easy and graceful.

Head maintains an upright, level position, not tilted to one side or the other

During the forward swing, the fist passes alongside the body but not across the chest

Shoulders back and chest opened up, enabling the rib cage to expand

Buttocks tucked under enable the pelvis to be correctly placed in a vertical position

Knees always relaxed and slightly flexed

Establish a brisk pace as the legs swing rhythmically out and forward

Stride gradually lengthens out as the rhythm is established

MEDITATION

Meditation is the process by which the mind is brought into the here and now. In doing this, mental storms are calmed and a profound inner source of clarity and quietness is uncovered. Meditation strengthens the body against stress and reveals the doorway to the soul. To meditate is to dwell in the presence of true peace. Step Three identifies the third ideal – peace of mind.

MEDITATION
ENJOYABLE EXERCISE
EINSTEIN ENERGY DIET

MEDITATION uses the language of enchantment. A complex tapestry woven from many threads, meditation is designed to resonate with the soul. You cannot unravel all the threads at once. Therefore, contemplate and live within each of the following meditations before you progress to the next one.

The eight meditations appeal to the entire range of inner aspiration. They awaken your sense of wonder. Do you remember how, as a child, your thoughts were quiet and still? How peaceful you felt gazing at the stars in the sky? Unfortunately, as adults, our thoughts are rarely that still. We are always busy planning, reflecting, worrying, strategizing, or even just thinking. The practice of meditation means simply learning to still your thoughts and enjoying the peace you felt as a child.

PEACE BEYOND IMAGINING
Meditation unchains your thoughts from both the past and future, and anchors them firmly in the present moment. As your restless thoughts begin to subside, the space between them slowly expands and you pass through the gateway of the soul to experience an inner peace beyond all your imagining.

Meditation supports and nurtures this peace as you begin to journey deep beneath the veil of chattering thoughts to hear the music of your soul. As you expand the quiet space between your thoughts, you restore inner harmony and balance, which fans the flame of your *healing force*. Every cell in your body comes alive and your soul sings with joy when you dwell in the presence of peace.

LYING POSITION FOR MEDITATION
Choose a quiet, warm, comfortable place where you can block out all distractions. It is often a good idea to unplug the phone. Stretch out on your back on the floor or your bed. Lie with your legs slightly apart and feet relaxed. Rest your hands by your sides with palms facing upwards and fingers relaxed. If necessary, use a blanket for warmth. Then, softly close your eyes and be still.

There is an inmost center in us all
Where truth abides in fullness.

ROBERT BROWNING

Head *faces upwards with the muscles of the forehead deeply relaxed*

Heels *are apart. Feet are naturally relaxed, with toes pointing outwards*

THE PRACTICE OF MEDITATION

The following eight meditations are consonant with traditional spiritual practices and beliefs.

Try to set aside your own special time each day for meditation. Early morning is often best, to help train your mind to relax. How long you meditate is up to you, but even the busiest person can meditate for five minutes. Your meditating time will increase as you learn to expand the space between your thoughts.

Work through the meditations in the order given. Spend about three days with each one before going on to the next. Remember the images and become very familiar with the words. Practice the meditation you are living with as often as you can: when you wake up in the morning, at the special time you set aside, at bedtime, and if you wake up during the night. Just experience peace as the space between the movement of your thoughts slowly expands.

You may find it helpful to have someone slowly and softly read the meditation to you at first. Ask them to *pause for quiet contemplation* for a few minutes and be silent between each passage. If stray thoughts come into your mind, acknowledge them and just let them drift gently away.

MEDICAL BENEFITS

Research shows that meditation enhances traditional medical care.

- The body's internal pharmacy and *healing force* is stimulated.
- The brain's electrical activity is calmed through an increase in brain waves associated with deep relaxation.
- The body's metabolic rate slows down, leading to more efficient oxygen consumption.
- Blood pressure and pulse rate both decrease, lessening the workload on the heart.

SITTING POSITIONS FOR MEDITATION

Wear easy loose-fitting clothes that let you sit comfortably and unrestricted, with good posture. Elongate your spine, neck and head gently upwards. Soften and relax your shoulders and allow them to come down and away from your ears. If you are sitting on the floor, cross your ankles and rest your hands in your lap with palms facing upwards. If you are sitting in a chair, uncross your arms and legs and rest your hands gently on your thighs.

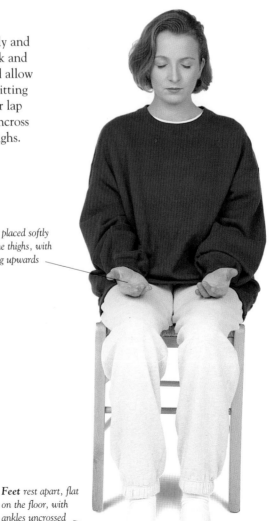

Hands *are placed softly on top of the thighs, with palms facing upwards*

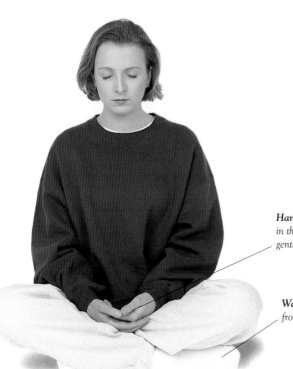

Hands *rest comfortably in the lap, with fingers gently relaxed*

Warm socks *keep feet from becoming chilled*

Feet *rest apart, flat on the floor, with ankles uncrossed*

SURRENDER TO PEACE

●

SURRENDERING TO PEACE WE FEEL THE PLEASURE OF STILLNESS
AND SILENT CONTEMPLATION. SURRENDERING TO PEACE WE
RETURN TO OUR NATURAL STATE. TO BE AT PEACE IS TO
BE IN HARMONY WITH EVERYONE AND EVERYTHING.
LET STILLNESS AND PEACE FLOW AROUND AND
WITHIN YOU AND FILL YOUR WHOLE BEING.

●

Find a quiet place and be comfortable. Gently close your eyes and begin now to quiet your thoughts in order to experience deep serenity and calm. Take seven deep, slow, even breaths. With each breath, relax each muscle in your body.

Begin by relaxing every single muscle of your face and neck. Then start to relax your shoulders, arms, hands, and fingers. Move down your body and relax your chest, your abdomen, and your back. Then relax your thighs, calves, feet, and toes. Relax.

Visualize now a warm, golden sun. Feel the rays of this golden sun flooding through your entire body, and feel your entire body filled with warm, golden, healing light.

PAUSE FOR QUIET CONTEMPLATION
*During this time dwell on the golden healing light
as you take each slow and even breath.*

Imagine the sun shining upon you as you stand in a serene country meadow. A glorious blue sky above and wildflowers of infinite shades carpet the earth beneath your feet. Breathe in nature's peace and beauty. See an artist's easel in front of you. See an empty canvas upon it. Have brushes and paints in your hands and become a marvelously talented artist. Begin to paint a picture of yourself as radiant and bathed in sunlight. Paint your face with a total expression of peace. Be a picture of peace. Feel yourself reflecting peace. See the entire canvas turn into a mirror in which you are a perfect reflection of peace.

Now turn away from the easel and walk through the meadow towards a lovely country cottage. See little rabbits scurrying about as you walk towards this cottage, so

PEACE IS IN THE STILLNESS OF YOUR THOUGHTS

welcoming and warm. The door is open and you enter, feeling comfortable and at peace. A cozy sofa beckons you to sit. Sit down, relax. See rays of sunlight streaming through the curtains and enjoy the warmth.

PAUSE FOR QUIET CONTEMPLATION
During this time dwell on the golden healing light as you take each slow and even breath.

Be aware of a comforting presence entering the room. Over your left shoulder, see a wise and wonderful person. See an ancient master of life. Sense that in the heart and soul of this master of life lies all the wisdom and beauty of the universe. Feel the infinite peace this master comes to share with you. Feel yourself in the presence of peace as the master sits down beside you and holds your hands. Listen to the master's message of peace. Listen … listen … listen.

Now the master must leave, departing with a gentle smile that assures you peace and inspiration will always be there for you in this country cottage. See yourself leaving now, returning to the meadow. See the colors of wildflowers before you. Admire nature's beauty and peace. Gazing at the wildflowers, feel the peace of nature uplift you. Peace fills your heart and the air you breathe. Peace surrounds you. Peace flows within you and fills your entire being.

PAUSE FOR QUIET CONTEMPLATION
During this time dwell on the golden healing light as you take each slow and even breath.

With your thoughts having been still for so long, begin to feel very refreshed and full of energy. Now take a nice slow, deep breath and slowly open your eyes. Come back to your waking consciousness.

LISTEN TO YOUR HEART AND BE AT PEACE

SURRENDER TO INNOCENCE

•

A CHILD'S MIND AND HEART ARE INNOCENT AND PURE. A
CHILD'S LOVE IS FREELY GIVEN. WHEN YOU LET GO OF
WORRY, RESENTMENT, AND FEAR YOU BECOME LIKE
A CHILD. WHEN YOU SURRENDER TO CHILDLIKE
INNOCENCE YOU BECOME PURE, FILLED WITH
THE FREEDOM OF HOPE, LOVE, AND JOY.

•

Find a quiet place and be comfortable. Gently close your eyes and begin now to quiet your thoughts in order to experience deep serenity and calm. Take seven deep, slow, even breaths. With each breath, relax each muscle in your body.

Begin by relaxing every single muscle of your face and neck. Then start to relax your shoulders, arms, hands, and fingers. Move down your body and relax your chest, your abdomen, and your back. Then relax your thighs, calves, feet, and toes. Relax.

Visualize now a warm, golden sun. Feel the rays of this golden sun flooding through your entire body, and feel your entire body filled with warm, golden, healing light.

PAUSE FOR QUIET CONTEMPLATION
*During this time dwell on the golden healing light
as you take each slow and even breath.*

Imagine yourself standing in a beautiful meadow filled with vibrant wildflowers. Watch the soft petals and leaves of the flowers dancing lightly on the gentle breeze of a warm and sunny day. See yourself lying down in the middle of this wonderful meadow, on a welcoming blanket of soft grass beneath you. Gaze at the mountains far away in the distance. Hear birds singing joyfully all around you. Feel happiness and joy in the air.

Watch as soft, white clouds drift slowly by above you. See a lovely rainbow forming across the wide, open sky. Observe the array of soft colors spanning the entire horizon. Concentrate on this rhapsody of soft color and just feel its warm light surrounding you, within and without. Let yourself bathe in the peace and tranquillity

INNOCENCE BRINGS FREEDOM TO YOUR SPIRIT

of nature's beauty. Feel happiness and joy filling your entire being. Experience the pure delight of being a child again while you are lying down peacefully in this meadow on a warm summer's day.

PAUSE FOR QUIET CONTEMPLATION
During this time dwell on the golden healing light as you take each slow and even breath.

As you are lying down in the meadow, beneath the soft colorful rainbow, imagine a beautiful golden key appearing at your side. Become aware that you have been given a sacred key that opens up your heart to happiness and love. Realize this key has always been waiting for you, but only peace and tranquillity bring it within your reach. Hold the key in both your hands. Now feel your heart open up and allow all the pains of your past to be released. See all your

hurtful memories rising above you, merging with the rainbow. Just let them go.

Feel unlimited happiness opening your heart. Feel unlimited love filling your heart. Let your heart open wider and wider, receiving unlimited happiness and love. Open your heart, and feel it expanding. Now feel happiness and love flowing throughout your entire body. Experience a deep inner joy filling your heart. Feel like a child, full of unlimited happiness and love.

PAUSE FOR QUIET CONTEMPLATION
During this time dwell on the golden healing light as you take each slow and even breath.

With your thoughts having been still for so long, begin to feel very refreshed and full of energy. Now take a nice slow, deep breath and slowly open your eyes. Come back to your waking consciousness.

OPEN UP YOUR HEART TO PURE DELIGHT AND JOY

SURRENDER TO JOY

●

WHEN YOU ARE ALIVE WITH JOY YOUR BODY, MIND, AND SPIRIT
ARE TRULY IN PERFECT BALANCE. INNER JOY REVIVES YOUR
HEALING FORCE AND UPLIFTS YOUR WHOLE BEING. EVEN
WHEN YOU JUST SMILE WITH JOY YOUR ENTIRE BODY
COMES ALIVE AND INSPIRES HAPPINESS, LOVE,
AND PEACE IN THE WORLD AROUND YOU.

●

Find a quiet place and be comfortable. Gently close your eyes and begin now to quiet your thoughts in order to experience deep serenity and calm. Take seven deep, slow, even breaths. With each breath, relax each muscle in your body.

Begin by relaxing every single muscle of your face and neck. Then start to relax your shoulders, arms, hands, and fingers. Move down your body and relax your chest, your abdomen, and your back. Then relax your thighs, calves, feet, and toes. Relax.

Visualize now a warm, golden sun. Feel the rays of this golden sun flooding through your entire body, and feel your entire body filled with warm, golden, healing light.

PAUSE FOR QUIET CONTEMPLATION
*During this time dwell on the golden healing light
as you take each slow and even breath.*

Completely relaxed now, feel as light and soft as a cloud. All your burdens disappear, and you are as light as a cloud. Imagine yourself relaxing softly on a cloud, like a heavenly pillow, unbelievably serene.

Let go of all your thoughts, all your worries and concerns. Just set them all free. Float, unburdened, on this soothing cloud. As you release your thoughts, you become lighter, floating ever more freely on this gently drifting cloud. Feel the warmth and softness of your cloud enfolding you, curving with the shape of your body. Feel yourself cushioned by this cloud.

As you drift in the tranquillity of the cloud, be aware of the heavenly blue sky surrounding you. See yourself surrounded by a soft blanket of blue tranquillity. Feel tranquillity surround you and fill you as you

RADIANT JOY GIVES HOPE AND LOVE TO ALL

continue to float on your cloud. Let your mind become tranquil, like the vast sky. See any interrupting thoughts drift away from you, in tiny thought-clouds, drifting away, until your mind is tranquil and still. Feel your mind becoming clearer and clearer, like the joyous sky around you.

PAUSE FOR QUIET CONTEMPLATION
During this time dwell on the golden healing light as you take each slow and even breath.

Now see your feather-light cloud illumined by the sunlight as it floats through the wide blue sky. As the sun's light reaches your cloud, it becomes luminous, shining with a golden glow. Feel the golden glow infusing your body with radiant joy. Imagine yourself floating on a cloud of pure joy. Feel the joy uplift you. As you continue to float, feel yourself becoming ever more joyful.

Feel yourself floating in joy. Experience a deep inner contentment. Feel it expanding with your every breath. Feel contentment and joy expanding within you as you rest peacefully on your cloud. Feel the power of love and joy to heal.

Now become aware of your cloud gently drifting to the ground. Let yourself float back to the ground and watch your cloud slowly rise into the sky. Feel how deeply content and peaceful you have become.

PAUSE FOR QUIET CONTEMPLATION
During this time dwell on the golden healing light as you take each slow and even breath.

With your thoughts having been still for so long, begin to feel very refreshed and full of energy. Now take a nice slow, deep breath and slowly open your eyes. Come back to your waking consciousness.

WITHIN YOU LIES AN INFINITE SOURCE OF JOY

SURRENDER TO FORGIVENESS

•

SURRENDERING TO FORGIVENESS, WE CAN TREAT OURSELVES GENTLY. SURRENDERING TO FORGIVENESS, WE CAN RELEASE OURSELVES FROM THE PAIN OF ANGER, SHAME, AND GUILT. AFFIRM YOUR WILLINGNESS TO BE FORGIVEN, AND TO FORGIVE, BY TAKING THIS IMPORTANT STEP ON THE PATH TO HEALING YOUR WHOLE SELF.

•

Find a quiet place and be comfortable. Gently close your eyes and begin now to quiet your thoughts in order to experience deep serenity and calm. Take seven deep, slow, even breaths. With each breath, relax each muscle in your body.

Begin by relaxing every single muscle of your face and neck. Then start to relax your shoulders, arms, hands, and fingers. Move down your body and relax your chest, your abdomen, and your back. Then relax your thighs, calves, feet, and toes. Relax.

Visualize now a warm, golden sun. Feel the rays of this golden sun flooding through your entire body, and feel your entire body filled with warm, golden, healing light.

PAUSE FOR QUIET CONTEMPLATION
During this time dwell on the golden healing light as you take each slow and even breath.

Now imagine yourself in a lovely, natural place, and see there a pool of warm, healing water. See other people sitting in this pool. As you gaze upon their faces, be aware that you are looking at loved ones from long ago, when you were very little. See them beckon you to come and be with them in this pool of warm, healing water.

Gently rest your head on the shoulders of your loved ones from long ago. Feel yourself being gently held by them, with great tenderness, and feel yourself being gently rocked by them, back and forth.

Now hear your loved ones tell you to begin each of your days with love. Fill each of your days with love. End each of your days with love. Continue to feel yourself being held and gently rocked by your loved ones from long ago. Realize how very much

you are loved. Accept the fact that you are completely forgiven. Completely and absolutely and totally forgiven. Approve of yourself and love being alive.

PAUSE FOR QUIET CONTEMPLATION
During this time dwell on the golden healing light as you take each slow and even breath.

Begin now to say farewell to all of your loved ones from long ago. Step out of the water and feel warm and dry. See standing before you a master of life who contains all of the wisdom of the entire universe in his heart and in his soul. Feel this master of life place your hands in his and listen carefully as he discusses with you your mission and purpose in this lifetime.

Hear the master of life tell you that in the stillness of your thoughts, you are with him at every moment. Hear him tell you

that in the peacefulness of your heart, your life's mission and purpose will be unveiled to you. Hear him tell you that in the still whisper of your heart, you will experience the deep sacredness of all life.

Now see the master begin to leave and wave farewell to you. Walk ahead and find yourself in a lovely country meadow on a summer's day. Feel the warmth of the air. Smell the sweetness of the flowers. Know the presence of God in every living thing.

PAUSE FOR QUIET CONTEMPLATION
During this time dwell on the golden healing light as you take each slow and even breath.

With your thoughts having been still for so long, begin to feel very refreshed and full of energy. Now take a nice slow, deep breath and slowly open your eyes. Come back to your waking consciousness.

HEARTFELT FORGIVENESS IS A BEAUTIFUL THING

SURRENDER TO LOVE

●

THE LOVE WE GIVE AND THE LOVE WE RECEIVE HAVE PROFOUND
EFFECTS ON THE PROCESS OF HEALING. LEARNING HOW TO
GIVE AND RECEIVE LOVE IS THE GREATEST LESSON AND
TASK IN LIFE. WHEN WE LEARN TO LOVE FREELY
AND WITHOUT ANY CONDITIONS, THEN WE
KNOW THAT LOVE ALONE CAN HEAL.

●

Find a quiet place and be comfortable. Gently close your eyes and begin now to quiet your thoughts in order to experience deep serenity and calm. Take seven deep, slow, even breaths. With each breath, relax each muscle in your body.

Begin by relaxing every single muscle of your face and neck. Then start to relax your shoulders, arms, hands, and fingers. Move down your body and relax your chest, your abdomen, and your back. Then relax your thighs, calves, feet, and toes. Relax.

Visualize now a warm, golden sun. Feel the rays of this golden sun flooding through your entire body, and feel your entire body filled with warm, golden, healing light.

PAUSE FOR QUIET CONTEMPLATION
*During this time dwell on the golden healing light
as you take each slow and even breath.*

See yourself walking in a country meadow on a warm summer's day. Follow the sound of gently flowing water until you come to a stream. Sit down on a boulder and begin to imagine a wonderful and inspirational event occurring in front of you. Imagine an event so wonderful and inspirational that the world may never be quite the same again. Actually become a part of this event and allow yourself to be carried away with inspiration and wonder.

Now allow the event to fade, and turn slightly on the boulder to face upstream. See before you a beautiful, serene waterfall. Watch its warm, gentle waters falling peacefully into a shallow, inviting pool. These waters offer love and forgiveness to all who enter. Place the images of all the people you know, who need your love, in

LOVE HAS THE POWER TO HEAL YOUR SOUL

these gentle waters. Also place the images of all the people you know, who are in need of your forgiveness, in these gentle waters. Include everyone from your present life and from your past to whom you wish to send your love and forgiveness. See them all bathed in these gentle, healing waters.

PAUSE FOR QUIET CONTEMPLATION
*During this time dwell on the golden healing light
as you take each slow and even breath.*

See the images of all the people who are in the healing waters begin to fade. Know they will receive the love and forgiveness you are sending. Now lift yourself up from the boulder and walk into the gentle stream yourself. Feel love and forgiveness wash gently over you. Become aware that the people to whom you sent your love and forgiveness are now sending their love and

forgiveness back to you. Take this feeling deep within you, to your very soul. Let the healing waters soothe and cleanse you. The waters purify your body, mind, and spirit. The waterfall whispers to you an eternal truth: if you cry just one tear, God will wipe away one thousand tears. Surrender to this truth. Surrender to love.

Emerge from the stream, letting the sun warm and dry you instantly as you walk once more through the colorful meadow.

PAUSE FOR QUIET CONTEMPLATION
*During this time dwell on the golden healing light
as you take each slow and even breath.*

With your thoughts having been still for so long, begin to feel very refreshed and full of energy. Now take a nice slow, deep breath and slowly open your eyes. Come back to your waking consciousness.

TO GIVE LOVE IS THE GREATEST GIFT OF ALL

SURRENDER TO TRUE PURPOSE

●

EXPAND YOUR AWARENESS OF LIFE'S MEANING AND PURPOSE.
BENEATH THE VEIL OF THOUGHTS LIES TRUE PERCEPTION.
YOUR SOUL IS CONNECTED TO THE INFINITE SOURCE OF
WISDOM AND TRUTH. TRUE PURPOSE IS REVEALED
IN THE ETERNAL STILLNESS OF MEDITATION
AND IN THE SILENCE OF THE SOUL.

●

Find a quiet place and be comfortable. Gently close your eyes and begin now to quiet your thoughts in order to experience deep serenity and calm. Take seven deep, slow, even breaths. With each breath, relax each muscle in your body.

Begin by relaxing every single muscle of your face and neck. Then start to relax your shoulders, arms, hands, and fingers. Move down your body and relax your chest, your abdomen, and your back. Then relax your thighs, calves, feet, and toes. Relax.

Visualize now a warm, golden sun. Feel the rays of this golden sun flooding through your entire body, and feel your entire body filled with warm, golden, healing light.

PAUSE FOR QUIET CONTEMPLATION
*During this time dwell on the golden healing light
as you take each slow and even breath.*

Imagine yourself sitting at the top of a lofty mountain. See a golden sun lighting up the mountainsides, warming and comforting you in its gentle glow. The mountainsides slope easily into a vast green valley beneath you, blanketed by a soft veil of mist. See the mist drift across the valley towards the horizon. Let your thoughts drift away with the mist. Now see more clearly the beauty that surrounds you. Experience a greater clarity of mind as your worries drift away.

PAUSE FOR QUIET CONTEMPLATION
*During this time dwell on the golden healing light
as you take each slow and even breath.*

Walk along a beautiful mountain path. See tree tops soaring towards the sky and hear birds filling the warm air with songs of joy. Just ahead lies a clearing where an ancient white marble library stands, glistening in

YOUR HEART KNOWS THE MEANING OF YOUR LIFE

the sunlight. Walk up the steps and see a kind and wise librarian, dressed in a flowing robe of white. The librarian takes your hand to guide you through rows and rows of ancient books. Among the books, one captures your attention. It is very old, bound in leather, with your name engraved in gold along its binding. Take the book from the shelf, follow the librarian to a wooden table, and sit down and open the book. On the opening page is a dedication, written just for you, that says: "Have faith that if you take one genuine step towards God, God will take one thousand steps towards you." Now turn to the next page. In a careful and beautiful hand is written the following message especially for you: "Begin each day with love, fill each day with love, and end each day with love."

Allow the messages you have just received to fill up the entire space of your heart and soul with each silent moment. Carry these comforting words with you in your heart and soul as you bid a warm farewell to the librarian. Walk along the mountain path once more, to the very top of the mountain where it overlooks the valley. Sense the truth and wisdom that your soul has revealed to you. Feel your heart expanding as you open up to your true purpose.

PAUSE FOR QUIET CONTEMPLATION
During this time dwell on the golden healing light as you take each slow and even breath.

With your thoughts having been still for so long, begin to feel very refreshed and full of energy. Now take a nice slow, deep breath and slowly open your eyes. Come back to your waking consciousness.

STILLNESS REVEALS WISDOM AND TRUTH

SURRENDER TO HEALING

•

UNLIMITED HEALING COMES FROM RECOGNIZING THAT YOU ARE
CONNECTED TO ALL THAT IS. THE EBB AND FLOW OF YOUR
MIND IS PART OF AN IMMENSE AND INFINITE OCEAN
OF LIFE. DEEPEN YOUR AWARENESS OF NATURE'S
ENERGY AROUND AND WITHIN YOU, AND
SURRENDER YOUR SELF TO HEALING.

•

Find a quiet place and be comfortable. Gently close your eyes and begin now to quiet your thoughts in order to experience deep serenity and calm. Take seven deep, slow, even breaths. With each breath, relax each muscle in your body.

Begin by relaxing every single muscle of your face and neck. Then start to relax your shoulders, arms, hands, and fingers. Move down your body and relax your chest, your abdomen, and your back. Then relax your thighs, calves, feet, and toes. Relax.

Visualize now a warm, golden sun. Feel the rays of this golden sun flooding through your entire body, and feel your entire body filled with warm, golden, healing light.

PAUSE FOR QUIET CONTEMPLATION
*During this time dwell on the golden healing light
as you take each slow and even breath.*

See yourself standing at the edge of the seashore. Look out to the far horizon and see the golden sun casting a warm color across the beautiful calm sea. Bask in the serenity of this wonderful day. Absorb its warmth, feeling yourself healed by its beauty. Now walk beside the sea, feeling the calm warm waters lapping at your bare toes and feet. Feel yourself being touched by the smooth, gentle, healing waters of the tide. Warm water softly caresses your toes and feet, rejuvenating and refreshing you, washing away weariness, sadness, and worry. Continue strolling peacefully along the edge of the shoreline, feeling warm, healing energy washing over your feet, soothing and healing you. The sea is gentle and calm, just tiny ripples of softly rolling waves. Watch small waves forming and

HEALING ENERGY EXISTS IN EVERY LIVING THING

merging back into the calm sea. Imagine yourself as a small wave connected with the vast ocean of life. Allow the soft warm current to soothe and heal you.

PAUSE FOR QUIET CONTEMPLATION
During this time dwell on the golden healing light as you take each slow and even breath.

Sit yourself down on the warm, dry sand and become aware of the presence of a wonderful master of life sitting beside you. Place your hands gently into the hands of the master, and feel wonderful healing energy flooding through your body – your muscles, your bones, your joints, your organs, your brain. Feel the healing energy fill you with vitality and health. Now hear the master of life inform you that it is time to forgive all individuals in your life and to forgive yourself. Feeling your hands in the master's hands, sense an overwhelming forgiveness flow through your entire being. Accept it totally and completely.

Bid farewell to the loving master of life now. Walk back to the edge of the shore and face the sunset and sea. As the ocean glistens beneath a golden light, feel the light filling your entire being. Feel yourself filled with healing light. As the powerful healing light of nature fills you, silently affirm and repeat: I am well … I am well.

PAUSE FOR QUIET CONTEMPLATION
During this time dwell on the golden healing light as you take each slow and even breath.

With your thoughts having been still for so long, begin to feel very refreshed and full of energy. Now take a nice slow, deep breath and slowly open your eyes. Come back to your waking consciousness.

LET THE POWER OF NATURE ENFOLD YOUR BEING

SURRENDER TO INNER STRENGTH

•

THE INFINITE SOURCE OF STRENGTH RESIDES DEEP WITHIN
YOU. WHEN IT IS NEEDED AT DIFFICULT PERIODS DURING
YOUR LIFE, UNLIMITED STRENGTH FLOWS FROM YOUR
SOUL. THE STRENGTH OF THE BODY CHANGES AND
DECLINES AS TIME PASSES, BUT THE STRENGTH
OF THE SOUL ENDURES INTO ETERNITY.

•

Find a quiet place and be comfortable. Gently close your eyes and begin now to quiet your thoughts in order to experience deep serenity and calm. Take seven deep, slow, even breaths. With each breath, relax each muscle in your body.

Begin by relaxing every single muscle of your face and neck. Then start to relax your shoulders, arms, hands, and fingers. Move down your body and relax your chest, your abdomen, and your back. Then relax your thighs, calves, feet, and toes. Relax.

Visualize now a warm, golden sun. Feel the rays of this golden sun flooding through your entire body, and feel your entire body filled with warm, golden, healing light.

PAUSE FOR QUIET CONTEMPLATION
*During this time dwell on the golden healing light
as you take each slow and even breath.*

Imagine yourself standing before a tall and stately tree. Look at the tree's branches, stretching towards the sky. See the sunlight as it glistens through the green leaves, forming a golden canopy of peace for you to sit beneath. Walk up to the tree and sit beneath it, resting comfortably against its sturdy trunk. Feel the sunlight streaming through the branches and leaves, bathing you in comfort and warmth. Watch the sunlight dancing on the leaves as they rustle in the delicate breeze. Except for the dancing leaves, everything is still around you. Feel the stillness that settles over this tranquil place. Feel quiet and at peace.

At the very center of the peace stands your tree. At peace with yourself and your surroundings, begin to feel your deep inner strength. All worries, all fears, all anxieties,

THE STRENGTH OF THE SOUL IS WITHOUT END

all burdens have disappeared, as if the arms of your tree had just picked them up and released them for you. Nothing remains to weaken your inner strength.

PAUSE FOR QUIET CONTEMPLATION
During this time dwell on the golden healing light as you take each slow and even breath.

Now feel your inner strength expanding within you. Become like the mighty tree you are resting against. Become a pillar of strength. Know that your soul is the core of your inner strength. Feel your strength expand from that place. Strength fills your heart and flows throughout your entire being. Feel this abiding strength within.

Now stand and face your tree. Look at its branches soaring skyward. Feel yourself soar with strength. Feel yourself uplifted. Now stand close to your tree and wrap your arms around its trunk. Feel infused with energy. Rest your cheek against its bark, breathing in its woodsy fragrance. The fragrance and bark remind you of God's presence in every living thing. Feel this presence in your heart, expanding within you, connecting you to the nature that surrounds you. Take a step back from the tree now, admiring the light dancing through the leaves. Feel the strength and serenity of nature's embrace. Feel renewed, your inner strength restored.

PAUSE FOR QUIET CONTEMPLATION
During this time dwell on the golden healing light as you take each slow and even breath.

With your thoughts having been still for so long, begin to feel very refreshed and full of energy. Now take a nice slow, deep breath and slowly open your eyes. Come back to your waking consciousness.

DE-ADDICTION

Addictions – particularly nicotine and alcohol – are energy thieves. They are toxic energy that disrupts the flow and balance of your natural energy. Addictions injure the body, enslave the mind, and suppress the capacity of the human spirit to experience joy. They ruin health, happiness, and life itself. Step Four identifies the fourth ideal – release from harmful substances.

De-addiction
Meditation
Enjoyable Exercise
Einstein Energy Diet

INDUCEMENTS to use substances that make you feel good capture a basic human need with relentless efficiency. Like the voice of a siren, clever advertising messages seduce you with visions of happiness and freedom from life's stress.

But once using such substances, your thoughts may easily become swayed by the pleasurable feelings they create. Your mind may begin to long for more, in order to feel good – or at least to not feel bad.

De-addiction is releasing yourself from harmful habits and substances. It requires a new sense of hardiness that will empower you to increase your resistance to stress and enjoy health into the new millennium.

TOXIC FOREIGN ENERGY

Recall that your body is a system of energy. The harmful substances you use to feel good – including refined sugar, alcohol, caffeine, chocolate, tobacco, and prescribed and illegal drugs – are also energy. All of these substances flow through your body and mind as toxic foreign energy, disrupting your natural life-energy.

Tremendous strain is thus placed on your *healing force* in its struggle to maintain harmony and balance. As ever increasing amounts of the substance are needed to experience the same good feeling, ever greater effort is required from your *healing force*. Then, wasted energy – in the form of worry, anger, fear, and other

toxic emotions – pours out of you in a chaos of directions. Now, vital energy, wastefully expended, is no longer available to help maintain equilibrium and health.

STRESS OVERWHELMS RESOLVE

Harmful substances are particularly devastating during times of stress. The currents of energy that stream through your whole being become polluted. Their free flow is dammed by the debris of alcohol, sugar, and other rocks and boulders.

You can turn harmful habits into healthful behavior by focusing your energy inward. Only then will you begin to feel the sense of wellness that parts the veils of addiction.

WHAT ADDICTION MEANS – THREE IDENTIFIABLE PHASES

PHASE ONE – DEPENDENCE
The need to feel good is an integral part of being human. Unhappy feelings attract us towards harmful substances, which at first delude our brain and make us feel better.

PHASE TWO – TOLERANCE
Our energy systems change with the natural rhythm of our lives. An adult in midlife may experience deepening gloom from the same amount of substance that once gave relief.

PHASE THREE – WITHDRAWAL
Our thoughts are overcome by the substances to which we are addicted. Therefore we need resolve, commitment, and trust in our inner healing force to release ourselves from them.

PHASE ONE – DEPENDENCE

Addiction is characterized by the fact of a harmful substance having the power to control you, instead of you controlling it.

The initial phase of addiction is called *dependence*. It develops when the body, in an effort to counteract the disruption to its energy flow, readjusts itself to incorporate the substance – toxic foreign energy.

As the readjustment occurs, the body becomes reliant on the toxic energy and generates thoughts that demand it *just to get going* or *just to feel right*. You need the substance now, *just to avoid feeling bad*.

Wisdom for Dependence

∿ The root cause of *dependence* is always the same, regardless of the substance used, including refined sugar, caffeine, illegal drugs, non-prescription medicines, alcohol, and chocolate. The root cause is the need to feel good.

∿ The common factor of such a need is feelings of insecurity, emptiness, and unhappiness.

∿ The cure is always serenity, inspired by feelings of gratitude, tranquillity, and love.

PHASE TWO – TOLERANCE

The pivotal phase of addiction is called *tolerance*. It occurs when the human energy system, your body, begins to need more and more of the same toxic foreign energy to achieve the same basic sensation.

The onset of this phase will vary according to certain factors, which may include age, body size, mental health, and genetic makeup.

Tolerance develops slowly but surely to reach ever higher levels. You need an increasing amount of the substance, *just to not feel bad*.

Wisdom for Tolerance

∿ Overcoming *tolerance* requires acknowledging that the substance is causing either physical, mental, or spiritual harm – or all three. It is essential to accept this fact.

∿ Energy systems reflect the ebb and flow of life. A mature adult may experience gloom from the same amount of substance that once generated happiness.

∿ Your *healing force* is always at work. Remembering this puts the healing process into perspective. You can strengthen your *healing force* by taking greater control of substances that disrupt its flow.

PHASE THREE – WITHDRAWAL

Withdrawal is addiction's third and final characteristic. The readjusted human energy system, having now incorporated toxic energy into its regular metabolism, experiences distress and *dis-ease* when deprived of the harmful substance.

Discomforting thoughts arise to remind you of the very pleasurable sensations once associated with the substance. The same thoughts also convey the notion that healing the addiction would be too painful and thus unjustifiable. With using such thoughts, *temptation proves stronger than willpower and control*.

Wisdom for Withdrawal

∿ The physical experience of *withdrawal* is in reality much less tortuous than most people have been conditioned to believe.

∿ With some addictions, such as alcohol, nicotine, and drugs, you cannot "think" your way out of them. Commitment is required.

∿ Commitment means setting a definite date to begin a healthier way of living. It means relying on a greater and higher power – your *healing force* – to get you through the process of de-addiction.

RELEASE FROM ENERGY THIEVES

HUMAN BEINGS have pursued gratification by chemical means for thousands of years. *How wonderful if chemicals could give us lasting happiness. How quick, how easy.* In our goal-oriented society, such thoughts can overwhelm the truth of values that have held good for generations – values that celebrate personal effort, gratitude, and love. It is almost as if the whole of our society is habituated or addicted, awash with substances that harm our bodies, dull our minds, and suppress our spirits. A majority are legal weekly, or daily, purchases. We toss candy, coffee, pastries, and ice cream into the shopping cart alongside fresh, live, and healthful foods without thought or care. Isn't it sad?

Personal responsibility, self-value, and reverence for life are the keys to gain release from substances that do you harm. Nothing helps more in overcoming habits or addictions than developing skills that enable you to cope with stress and threats to your confidence and self-esteem. Then, substances once needed to make you happy or give you a *quick fix* lose their attraction and power.

REFINED SUGAR

Refined sugar offers only calories without vitamins, minerals, other nutrients, or fiber. In children, it contributes to learning difficulties, hyperactivity, and cavities in teeth. In adults, it contributes to obesity, heart disease, and diabetes, and causes mood swings and fatigue.

Ordinary table sugar – found in candy, pastries, cookies, ice cream, soda, breakfast cereals, and a host of sweetened foods – changes your natural life-energy balance. So also does sugar in other forms – sucrose, dextrose, and honey. Refined sugar robs energy. Remind yourself that a craving for sugar is driven mostly by clever advertising, lack of exercise, and emotional distress.

∼ *Satisfy your taste buds with fresh fruits and juices. They are packed with valuable nutrients that will help your body to fight infections. Their natural sugar content boosts energy levels and stabilizes mood swings.*

CHOCOLATE

Cravings for this combination of sugar, fat, and caffeine appear to be linked with brain chemistry. There is no other substance that produces the feeling that some characterize as euphoria. Remind yourself that you do not need chocolate to feel confident, empowered, and strong.

∼ *A small amount satisfies physical cravings, but not emotional needs.*

CAFFEINE

This chemical, especially as found in coffee, is more widely used than any other stimulant in the world. It is used to socialize with friends or family, but mostly just to get going in the morning, or to revive you at any time of day.

Caffeine is extremely disruptive to the human energy system. In pepping you up, it causes the heart to beat faster and blood pressure to rise. It is a common cause of heart palpitations, indigestion, frequent urination, headache, restlessness, anxiety, and insomnia.

Withdrawal symptoms can be countered by drinking half your usual amount of tea, coffee, and cola drinks every other day.

∼ *Remember the wisdom inherent in moderation in all things. Two cups of coffee or three cups of tea is a reasonable daily limit. Herbal tea, fresh juices, or water are best of all.*

REFINED SUGAR

CHOCOLATE

COFFEE BEANS

NONPRESCRIPTION MEDICINES

Year in, year out, billions of pills and oceans of liquid medicines are manufactured to relieve symptoms of anxiety, indigestion, insomnia, and pain, and to control weight.

These chemicals are generally sedatives or stimulants, which dull or intoxicate the mind and disrupt the natural balance of your body.

Exercise, yoga, good nutrition, and treatments such as *therapeutic massage* and *acupuncture* that seek to rebalance energy can effectively relieve many of life's aches, pains, and common ailments.

ILLEGAL RECREATIONAL DRUGS

Mood-changing chemicals such as marijuana and cocaine cannot be justified for individuals who aspire to ideal levels of balance. Uppers, downers, and hallucinogens have greater power to seduce you than any other substance, while at the same time disrupting your energy balance – sometimes severely.

Marijuana produces apathy and interferes with memory function. Cocaine, in addition to producing alarming levels of overexcitement and overstimulation, has serious physical effects including allergic reactions and sudden death. Drugs can so easily begin to control you, rather than you controlling them.

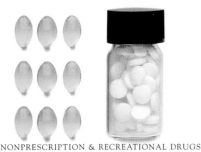

NONPRESCRIPTION & RECREATIONAL DRUGS

HEALING ALCOHOL ADDICTION

Emotional distress is the cause of problem drinking. If you are having a problem, it is important to face the truth, and dramatically curtail the amount and frequency of your alcohol use. If you are unable to do so, it is vital to stop drinking entirely, before the problem gets out of control.

The most successful treatment for alcohol addiction is to escape from negative self-judgment. Therefore, it is vital to build up your strengths on a day-to-day basis through small amounts of self-discipline, with exercise, yoga, meditation, healthy food, and an ethical lifestyle.

Stimulating Wellness

- Your *healing force* is working whether you ask it to or not.
- Cultivating healthful, soulful habits will bolster your natural life-energy.
- Doing so unleashes a boundless resource that will empower and strengthen you.
- Your strengths will increase over time, so you can handle major stressful events, negative emotions, and threats to your confidence and self-esteem.

Regaining Control

- Do whatever it takes to regain control – *anything that might help that you are not doing now.*
- Overcome denial. Seek social support from family and friends. Avoid drinking environments and friends. Attend Alcoholics Anonymous. Talk to a therapist, physician, minister, or rabbi.
- Recite the Serenity Prayer (see below) often. There is magic in its timeless wisdom.
- Don't wait to hit rock bottom.

Grant me the serenity to accept

the things I cannot change,

The courage to change the things I can,

And the wisdom to know the difference.

THE SERENITY PRAYER

RELEASE FROM NICOTINE

Smokers require special understanding because their minds have become enslaved by nicotine. Nicotine is a powerful drug that causes smokers to think that they cannot survive without smoking. Such thoughts are not the truth. You can break the shackles of your addiction to nicotine. For your sake, and for the sake of people who love you, save your life by making up your mind to quit smoking. Resolve now to follow this treatment.

A CIGARETTE is a system for the instant delivery of nicotine to your brain and toxic energy to your body. With each puff of a cigarette, a lethal combination of chemicals that includes arsenic and hydrogen cyanide is delivered into your body.

THE VOYAGE TO FREEDOM
You will probably be familiar with thoughts such as *I definitely want to quit* and *I'm absolutely going to try to quit* if you have considered quitting at any time. Just as familiar is your mind's response – *I know I should quit, but quitting is just too painful.*

Nicotine-drenched thoughts like these overwhelm your resolve. It is as if your mind were saying to you, *Nicotine makes me feel good. I want more. Give it to me.* Thus, your own thoughts predict and cause failure.

Quitting causes considerably less physical discomfort than what you experience during a common cold. Remember, nicotine can be out of your system in seventy-two hours.

The treatment begins three days before you have your last cigarette. Follow the instructions on the page opposite and continue with *Voyage to Freedom* on pages 122 and 123.

> Come to the edge,
>   he said: they said –
>   we are afraid.
> Come to the edge,
>   he said: they came.
> He pushed them
>   and they flew.
>
> GUILLAUME APOLLINAIRE

ARE YOU ADDICTED TO NICOTINE?

If you answer yes to three or more of the five questions below, you are addicted to nicotine.

- Do you smoke within 30 minutes of waking in the morning?
- Is the first cigarette of the day your most important?
- Do you smoke more than a pack of cigarettes a day?
- Do you smoke when you are ill or otherwise confined to bed?
- Do you find it difficult to refrain from smoking in places like movie theaters where it is forbidden?

QUITTING SIGNIFICANTLY IMPROVES HEALTH

Within 20 minutes of quitting, your blood pressure drops to the level that is the normal state for your body without nicotine.

Within 20 minutes of quitting, your resting pulse drops to the rate that is the normal state for your body without nicotine.

Within 2 weeks to 3 months of quitting, your lung function increases as much as 30% and your blood circulation becomes more efficient, making breathing and walking much easier.

Within 1 month to 9 months of quitting, coughing, sinus congestion, and shortness of breath all decrease. Proper function returns to your lungs, enabling them to fight infection. You feel generally less fatigued. Your levels of energy and stamina increase.

Within 1 year of quitting, your risk of heart attack is reduced by 50%.

Within a few years of quitting, your risk of developing life-threatening diseases – coronary heart disease and cancer of the mouth, throat, esophagus, and lungs – is reduced nearly to that of a nonsmoker.

MAKE UP YOUR MIND TO QUIT SMOKING

ONLY ONE STEP is needed for you to break the shackles of your nicotine addiction – just be willing to *make up your mind to quit*. It's easy *once you make up your mind*. Imagine you are planning a One-week Voyage to Freedom. Preparing three days before will ensure smooth sailing. *First –*

∿ Switch your usual cigarette brand to one that contains less nicotine and tar.

∿ Arrange to secure nicotine gum or patches (or other replacement) if you wish to use them.

∿ Get used to taking a daily multivitamin and mineral supplement that contains no less than 1000 mg of vitamin C (add extra if necessary).

∿ Set your definite Quit Smoking Date no later than ten days from today. Record this date by writing it on the contract at right. Then below it, write the date of the day that is three days before. Finally, sign your Contract for Life.

> ### CONTRACT FOR LIFE
> I hereby vow on my honor
> and integrity, and on all that
> I hold dear, that I will quit
> smoking forever no later
> than ten days from today.
>
> QUIT SMOKING DATE
> _____
> THREE DAYS BEFORE DATE
> _____
> YOUR SIGNATURE
> _____
> WITNESS'S SIGNATURE
> _____

THREE DAYS BEFORE

In making up your mind to quit, in signing your Contract for Life, you have taken the first and most vital step to starting a new life. A life in which you will take responsibility for your own health destiny. A life in which you are no longer a slave to nicotine. Now, it is time to get ready for your One-week Voyage to Freedom. It is time to confirm your declared resolve that very soon you will never smoke again. *Today –*

• Inform everyone you love, and who loves you, of your decision to quit smoking forever, and ask for their help and support.

TWO DAYS BEFORE

For each of the seven days of your voyage, plan more time for exercise and pleasurable activities with non-smoking friends. Stock up on fresh fruits and vegetables, sugarless hard candy, sugarless chewing gum, and cinnamon and black licorice sticks. *Today and also tomorrow –*

• Smoke only outside. Do not smoke in your car.

• Drink copious amounts of water.

• Make a concerted effort to clean your nails, hair, teeth, and every part of your body. Consider using a gentle herbal laxative if you are at all constipated.

ONE DAY BEFORE

Anticipate that your resolve may waver, and be ready to experience thoughts such as *I can't quit smoking because I'm addicted*. Strategies to help overcome stress are especially important at this time. *Today –*

• Dramatically decrease your use of caffeine and alcohol.

• Eat abundant amounts of fresh fruits and vegetables.

• Have your last cigarette ever.

• Throw away ashtrays, cigarette lighters, and remaining cigarettes.

• Take a long, brisk walk outdoors.

• Read the Serenity Prayer on page 123 and recite it over and over.

ONE-WEEK VOYAGE TO FREEDOM

THIS EXTRAORDINARY treatment has just five ingredients. Each ingredient represents a step towards ridding your body and mind of nicotine. With no exceptions, you must take all of the five steps, *not just some of them*, for each of seven days.

All of the nicotine in your system will be gone in three days. You will become a nonsmoker in just one week – with much less physical and mental discomfort than you experience during a common cold. Use this treatment to start a new life today.

MEDITATION & PRAYER

• Meditate first thing each morning, using whichever meditation you wish (see *Meditation*, pages 98–115).
• Recite the therapeutic *Serenity Prayer* (far right) softly and out loud at least three times a day, each day, and especially when waking up.
• Use the clinically proven *Emergency Stress Meditation* if you severely crave a cigarette (see box directly below).

ENJOYABLE EXERCISE & EASY YOGA

• Exercise throughout the day. A brisk walk in the morning, afternoon, and evening is ideal (see *Wellness Walking*, pages 96–97).
• Get out of breath by doing jumping jacks or briskly walking up and down flights of stairs.
• Practice yoga each morning (see *Wellness Yoga*, pages 84–95). Pay special attention to yoga ethics to reinforce your resolve to quit smoking.

EATING, DRINKING, & SNACKING

• Eat sensibly and avoid gaining excess weight by staying on the upper five rungs of the *Food Energy Ladder* (see page 59). Especially, have lots of fresh fruits and fruit juices – and not much else – until noon.
• Drink *huge* amounts of water or nonsweetened drinks without caffeine (fruit juices, herbal teas) to flush nicotine out of your body more quickly.
• Snack throughout the day, to keep your hands, lips, and mouth busy, on crunchy raw vegetables, breadsticks, crackers, popcorn, nuts, seeds, or raisins. Never be without sugarless gum, cinnamon sticks, and/or black licorice sticks.

CHANGES IN ROUTINE & ENVIRONMENT

• Abstain completely from alcohol this week.
• Eliminate coffee or reduce coffee intake.
• Spring-clean your car and home.
• Avoid acquaintances who smoke cigarettes.
• Prohibit smoking in your home.
• Choose to frequent places where smoking is prohibited.
• Take a shower when you wake up if you have an urge to smoke.
• Avoid stressful situations.
• Hold the telephone to the ear opposite the one you generally use.
• Don't get angry. Breathe deeply, count to ten, take a walk.

EMERGENCY STRESS MEDITATION

• Recall the most important reason for your decision to stop smoking and remember your commitment, contract, and sacred oath.

• With your eyes closed or open, take seven deep breaths, while defying the urge by saying silently: *This urge will not last more than 20 seconds and then I will be absolutely fine.*

• If necessary, also silently repeat, over and over: *I have strength – I have strength – I have strength.*

• You will receive the strength you need.

STEP 5

KINDNESS TOWARDS OTHERS & YOURSELF

• Perform one good deed or random act of kindness at least once each day. This can involve someone you know, or someone you haven't even met, such as getting groceries for a neighbor, teaching a skill, donating money to a charity, giving food or blankets to a homeless person, and so on.

• Schedule a pleasurable activity for yourself at least once each day this week, especially in the evening. Your evening walk could be followed by writing a letter to a friend you've lost touch with, reading a special book, buying new scent or cologne, listening to wonderful music, going to a good movie, getting a massage, visiting a nonsmoking friend or relative, and so on.

Grant me the serenity to accept
the things I cannot change,
The courage to change the things I can,
And the wisdom to know the difference.

THE SERENITY PRAYER

PREVENTING A RELAPSE

YOU BECAME an ex-smoker the very moment you made up your mind to eliminate smoking as an option, forever. You signed your *Contract for Life* and took the *Voyage to Freedom* to start anew. You have taken enormous personal responsibility for yourself, and shown great love for people who love and care for you. Feeling amazement at what you have achieved is natural. Congratulations on saving your life. Now proceed onwards with your ascent of the Pyramid of Human Aspiration.

Individuals who are habituated or addicted to harmful substances are engaged in a battle for their lives. This is especially true for nicotine addiction. Each year, smoking kills more people than AIDS, alcohol, illegal drugs, automobile accidents, and homicides combined. Second-hand smoke is causing respiratory illness in billions of children and infants. Smoking is a worse threat to humanity than bubonic plague, appropriately called the *black death*.

Preventing a Relapse addresses the continuing battle against nicotine. If you are addicted to a substance other than nicotine, consider how you might adapt the wisdom here to your personal situation.

TRIPWIRES & TRIGGERS

Many feelings and activities in the daily life of a smoker are linked to lighting up a cigarette. These are a few of the ways in which you once fashioned your life with cigarettes.

FEELINGS LINKED TO SMOKING
Worry. Excitement. Curiosity. Fear. Despondency. Anxiety. Frustration. Anger. Loneliness. Disappointment. Boredom. Anticipation.

ACTIVITIES LINKED TO SMOKING
Waking up. Going to the bathroom. Showering. Drinking coffee. Shaving. Applying makeup. Eating. Watching television. Driving your car. Having sex. Drinking alcohol. Using the phone. Going to bed.

THREE PILLARS OF VICTORY

The relapse prevention aspect of de-addiction is crucially important in the battle against nicotine, and especially so during times of stress. Although nicotine is out of your body, nicotine-drenched thoughts persist in your memory for many years. The three pillars of victory provide simple, effective strategies for continuing your defense.

Effective Time Management

∾ The *first pillar of victory* is to be aware of times when you are either engaged in activities or experiencing feelings that once made you reach for a cigarette.
∾ Then, find something else to do or think about, or face down the craving with the realization that it will last only 20 seconds.

Education & Understanding

∾ The *second pillar of victory* is to understand that your physical addiction is over. Thoughts like *I really need a cigarette* are merely disruptions of mental energy.
∾ Physical activity quickly resets this energy imbalance. Do yoga breathing (see page 84) at once and try to go outside for a walk.

Personal Resolve

∾ The *third pillar of victory* is to understand that you set free the power of your *healing force* once you truly made up your mind to quit smoking. Nothing on earth can shatter your resolve.
∾ Ascend and remember, *In any thing great or small – never, never, never give in except to convictions of honor and good sense.*

> Smoking is a custom harmful to the brain, dangerous to the lungs, and in the black fume thereof, nearest resembling the horrible Stygian smoke of the pit that is bottomless.
>
> JAMES I OF ENGLAND, 1604

BUILDING ON YOUR SUCCESS

You have worked hard to become a nonsmoker. At times, it may seem difficult to believe that you can keep it up. Recognize your achievement and challenge yourself to build on your success. Acknowledge, prepare, and reward yourself. You will be surprised at what strengths you have.

1 **Acknowledge Yourself.** List the 3 most important reasons that you quit. Alongside each, comment on how you feel about yourself now.

2 **Prepare Yourself.** List the circumstances or emotions that might trigger your desire to smoke. Alongside, list a distracting activity.
• family quarrel: *take a wellness walk* (see pages 96–97)
• job-related crisis: *recite the Serenity Prayer* (see page 123)
• friends offer a cigarette: *ask them if they need help to quit smoking*

3 **Reward Yourself.** List ways to reward your success – and to celebrate your savings from not buying cigarettes – at the end of each month. *Examples* take someone you love to a good nonsmoking restaurant; recreate a magical shared experience; give flowers to a special friend.

BUILDING SELF-ESTEEM

Self-esteem reflects feelings of personal worthiness. These feelings are more a result of current behavior than of past fortunes or misfortunes. What is done today, using the gifts of heart and mind, is what matters. Personal integrity and ethical living are the most reliable barometers of self-esteem. Step Five identifies the fifth ideal – goodness, confidence, and inner strength.

SELF-ESTEEM
DE-ADDICTION
MEDITATION
ENJOYABLE EXERCISE
EINSTEIN ENERGY DIET

Having self-esteem means that you feel good about yourself, worthy of health, happiness, love, and forgiveness. Self-esteem allows you full enjoyment of life's beauty, inspires a willingness to care about yourself – is the spark of confidence you need to meet life's challenges. Self-esteem is extremely powerful medicine to rebalance the energy of body, mind, and spirit.

THE BASIS OF SELF-ESTEEM

Our capacity for reflection is what sets human beings apart from other animals. We reflect on who we are, on our inner resources, and on how we can lead more meaningful lives. Reflecting on fundamental matters of this kind is the uniquely human characteristic that determines and underlies our level of self-esteem. It causes us to ask ourselves how well we deal with other people and with our relationships; whether we have integrity and are worthy of respect; and whether we are truly deserving of love and forgiveness.

In still reflection, when we listen to the whispers of our hearts, these questions provide the answers that form the basis of our self-esteem. If we hear positive responses, we feel confident of our inner strength and the ability to cope with every facet of life. Our innate knowledge that we can not merely survive, but also rise through difficulties and – in so doing – grow in goodness and love, is upheld and confirmed. Building self-esteem therefore generates self-fulfilling expectations that help us lead more loving, caring lives.

AFFIRMING YOUR GOODNESS

The philosopher, Plato, perceived the truth of eternity when he saw, with perfect vision, that a supreme *beauty* breathed human beings into life. He acknowledged this beauty as a sacred force, called it *God*, and named it *the Good*. Insightfully, he concluded that our soul's purpose is to ascend to the Good by glorifying nature and loving one another. An immutable ideal springs from these revelations – the *Ideal of the Good*.

BUILDING SELF-ESTEEM – GOODNESS, CONFIDENCE, & INNER STRENGTH

OVERCOMING DESPONDENCY
The deep ocean of turmoil called despair is illumined by turning up the light that is hidden within your soul – see pp.128–129.

A CONSTELLATION OF SOULS
Wellness, healing, and joy spring from your soul when you realize that you are connected to every other soul – see pp.130–131.

GAINING SELF-CONFIDENCE
A flexible, balanced mind allows confidence to soar, enabling you to become the person you were created to be – see pp.132–133.

FINDING PURPOSE IN LIFE
Action – governed by a sense of sacredness – works in harmony with nature and brings clarity to your purpose – see pp.134–135.

STRIVING FOR THE GOOD

Ascending this step of the Pyramid of Human Aspiration needs effort to overcome any feelings of futility that may obstruct your path. Work is required in order to break out of indecision and fear of hurt, failure, and the unknown. You are striving now for the Ideal of the Good. You can begin by offering your kindness or service to others each day. Soon, you will find that your potential for goodness has no end, and with this is given the potential for boundless health, because the energy of your whole self responds to goodness in healing ways. There is no source of self-esteem greater than the Good.

PARTING THE VEILS

Since the age of Plato in the fourth century BC, *almost all commentary about virtue and love has been drawn from his revelations that goodness, beauty, and love are the best work of the soul. Human glory fades with time, yet the Ideal of the Good shines undimmed behind the veils of the physical world, forever able to be rekindled as the moral basis of our being.*

Those who know distances out to the
outermost stars are astonished
when they discover the magnificent
space in their own heart.

RAINER MARIA RILKE

OVERCOMING DESPONDENCY

UNRESOLVED emotional burdens imposed on a stressed body act as a trigger for prolonged periods of despondency. With such emotions, you feel isolated on an island in the midst of an ocean of turmoil that is called *despair*. The remedy is to search in the darkness for even the tiniest flicker of light. The way out of the darkness is to turn up the light hidden within your soul. Sometimes, we must come very close to that darkness in order to perceive how very near the light we really are.

People are like stained
glass windows.
They sparkle and shine
when the sun is out,
But when the darkness
sets in, their true
beauty is revealed
Only if there is a light
from within.

DR. ELISABETH KÜBLER-ROSS

All forms of despondency – which may come from grief, anger, worry, loss, disability, fear, frustration, or other causes – are signs of spiritual sickness as well as sickness of body and mind. Despondency indicates an imbalance or lack of energy on all three levels.

Recharging your energy can help to restore balance and release you from the grip of despondency. It is as if you are inviting hope to come into your life again. To find hope, you must simply invite life in.

A DIVINE PRESENCE
If your soul is in turmoil, you need to bathe its darkness with your own inner light. Accumulated pain, sad memories, failed expectations, and old hurts respond remarkably well to this *soul treatment*. Step by step, you can learn how to live your life in order to experience joy instead of just to avoid hurt and pain.

To initiate this treatment means casting off all intellectual pretense and contemplating the presence of a sacred force within you. Anyone who can reach beyond information and intellect can fathom the truth that *all life is sacred*, and use this to overcome despondency and gloom. *We do our best to disprove the fact, but the fact remains: Man is as divine as nature, as infinite as the void.*

Hold on to these words of novelist and essayist, Aldous Huxley. Even use them while meditating at times when darkness threatens to engulf your path towards the light.

Set sail, then, away from the eye of the storm into the refuge of your soul. Set sail on a voyage that will take you from despondency to life and hope. The *empowering exercise* at right is a focus for the strategies further explained here.

MAKE READY TO SET SAIL
Overcoming despondency requires work – especially if you feel cut off from hope, and have lost sight of your inner light. Your goal is clear. Now, we shall define the path with strategies that you must follow with strong resolve. This soul treatment consists of *six key ingredients*.

ESTABLISHING A ROUTINE
Fashion your life around these six keys to establish a new routine.

Appropriate Selfishness is the *first key*. When you place all else above your own well-being, you miss the vital sense of *completion*. Bringing closure to a project, or reconciling a relationship, generates feelings of wholeness and nurture. Cultivate appropriate selfishness by taking necessary time to care for yourself. It is an essential element of life.

TWO SIDES OF THE UNIVERSE

A *Feeling of Gratitude* is the *second key* to overcoming despondency.

Einstein believed that the most important question to ask yourself is whether the universe is friendly or unfriendly. The way you answer this question each day affects your life more than any other decision you will ever make. Just counting our blessings is sometimes enough to reaffirm our strength.

BOOST YOUR ENERGY

The journey towards life and hope needs a special boost of energy.

Walking, Strolling, & Doing Yoga is the *third key*. Outdoor exercise is the surest path to new and greater energy. Walk in surroundings that please you, and notice them. Also, balance your energy with yoga.

Nurturing Food is the *fourth key*. Choose really fresh foods and take a daily comprehensive nutritional supplement. Avoid energy thieves like alcohol, caffeine, and sugar.

A Sense of Humor is the *fifth key*. Seek out light-hearted people. See a slapstick movie, or read a funny book. Truly smiling can help melt away gloom. But take note. A *true smile* ensues only from pleasure or humor that begins in your heart.

Meditation & Affirmation is the *sixth key*. The production of your body's natural feel-good chemicals (neuropeptides) is enhanced with daily meditation. These chemicals instill a sense of greater peace and tranquillity into your life. Deepen this sense by creating affirmations. These silent thoughts are songs to uplift your soul – sweet music that you can sing throughout the day.

EMPOWERING EXERCISE TO DISPEL FEELINGS OF HOPELESSNESS & GLOOM

Years ago, a popular song reminded us that *Life can be so sweet, on the sunny side of the street*. Set aside about ninety minutes each day to live life on the sunny side, following the six keys of your soul treatment.

1 Begin to set your priorities straight by helping to complete a project, or by reconciling a relationship that you have left dangling. Record your priorities here. Review them at least once a week.

....

....

....

2 List the 10 things that you feel most glad about – and most grateful for – in your life. Review the list daily, and change it as you wish.

....

....

....

3 Walk briskly for at least 20 minutes a day, then stroll for at least another 10 minutes while being intently aware of nature and your surroundings. Practice your yoga routine daily (pages 83–95).

4 Build your strength and balance your energy by eating live foods from the upper 5 rungs of the Ladder (page 59). Eliminate or significantly reduce your use of alcohol, caffeine, and other addictive substances.

5 Practice *true smiling*. Look in a mirror. Contract your cheek muscles until you can see your molars. Raise your eyebrows so you feel much taller. Then, laugh heartily at yourself and the world.

6 Stimulate your healing force with daily meditation. Especially, use *Surrender to Joy* (pages 104 & 105). Use affirmations such as *I have strength, I am loved, God loves me* to recharge your energy and hope.

In the depths of winter, I
finally learned that within me
there lay an invincible summer.

ALBERT CAMUS

A CONSTELLATION OF SOULS

OUR HUMAN LIVES span time and space, just like the glittering bodies of the Milky Way, connected with other human lives and souls. We contain multitudes – multitudes of opportunities to make healing or hurtful choices, using our gifts to build up or tear down, to bring goodness and love into the world or sully it with violence and hate. Self-esteem soars when we realize that our soul is entwined with the fabric of the universe, defining the existence of so many other souls.

Unlimited wellness and joy spring from our souls when we realize our connectedness with all that exists, with all that ever was, and with all that will be. This recognition, that each individual has a unique place in the world and is connected to it in a special way, promotes feelings of deep contentment which in turn inspire inner strength and healing.

MOMENT OF REVELATION
Healing begins to follow – even if the awareness of being connected passes only as a brief glimpse for a flickering moment. The revelation that we are all part of one another, that what we touch touches others, is captured in the poetic language of William Blake: *To see the world in a grain of sand, and heaven in a wild flower … Hold infinity in your hand, and eternity in an hour.*

Thus, your soul exists within a constellation of souls, where each soul touches and shapes the life of every other that shares its world.

THE GREAT HUNTER, ORION
Each star of Orion shines brilliantly alone, yet the spectacular light of this constellation comes from shining as a whole body. Human beings are similarly connected. Each individual life is unique, but our relationships with friends and family, people we barely know, and others we have yet to meet, bring us alive, and make us shine with purpose, meaning, and definition.

130

BEYOND THE CONFINES OF SELF

Grasping this beautiful truth gives us the courage to step beyond the limits of our own selves, where ego casts its shadows of selfishness and pride. Then, reverence for life and respect for each other flourish and develop into the invincible bonds of love that hold us together.

MAKING CIRCLES OF LIFE

An easy exercise helps in realizing your sense of connectedness.

Go outdoors and find a pool of still water. Or just fill a wide bowl with water. Drop a pebble into the water, and observe how concentric circles ripple outwards from where you dropped the pebble, in waves. These concentric waves are linked by ever-expanding waves of energy that you set in motion just by the act of dropping the pebble.

Now, visualize that you are that pebble, and that all the souls who surround you, near and far, are all interrelated, and expanding ever outwards from your soul.

YOUR OWN CONSTELLATION

This exercise helps in realizing that your place in the world is unique.

Draw a circle, representing your soul, in the center of a large sheet of paper. Then, write the names of all the people who share your love, depend on you, and on whom you depend in circles radiating out from your soul. Put names of friends and acquaintances, and of people from your past, in wider circles that fan ever outwards. Finally, visualize a whole galaxy, in which each person you have recorded is placed at the center of their own constellation.

TIME WITH NATURE

∽

Nature provides us with significant reminders of how intricately all life is woven together. Plan time with nature each day to deepen your sense of belonging in the world.

- Lie down on soft grass on a warm day. Smell the earth. Hear the hum of insects.
- Discover a perfect spider web.
- Sit quietly beside the ocean or by a river. Observe how the water dances and moves in ever-changing patterns.
- Watch the sun rise on a frosty winter morning.
- Go walking on a breezy day. Enjoy the sensation of wind blowing on your body and through your hair.
- Notice how new plants push up through the ground in spring, growing bigger and stronger week by week.
- Walk in the woods or among trees when leaves are falling. Hear the crunch of leaves, the snap of twigs. Feel the earth spring under your feet.

REVERENCE FOR LIFE

As we would respect our own mother, so too should we respect Mother Earth. Respect for the environment fosters reverence for life, in our neighborhoods as well as in the natural world. Honoring and feeling connected to the universe unclouds our vision, allowing us full recognition of ourselves as spiritual beings.

To live according to nature is
To live according to man's whole nature, not just a part of it –
To reverence the divinity within as the sole governor of his actions.

MARCUS AURELIUS ANTONINUS | *131*

GAINING SELF-CONFIDENCE

SELF-CONFIDENCE is the energy of self-esteem in motion. Its source is infinite, internal, born within us and nurtured (if sometimes neglected) by others throughout our childhood. Some people have wonderful early years, and others do not. In adult life, however, self-confidence is generated not by what others are willing to do for us, but by what we are willing to do for ourselves. Then, the sound of aspirations you had before you were told they were impossible rings out like a clear bell.

A flexible and balanced mind can recognize the attitudes that led to contradictory behavior in the past. No matter what you have done, no matter what hurtful experience you have been through, when you take personal responsibility for renewing yourself as the very best person you can be, your whole being will strive to increase your confidence, and to help you love yourself.

Accepting this is the first step in creating new ways of thinking that will enable you to change and grow, unfolding multiple layers of identity until the self that you were created to be emerges. Ramakrishna, Hindu yogi, offered this sage advice: *The winds of grace blow all the time. All we need do is set our sails.*

THE STRONG ANCHOR OF SELF

Self-confidence reflects the feeling that you are deeply anchored, not likely to be blown off course when fortune whistles a stormy wind. To gain such confidence, you need to recognize what you are – *as well as what you are not.* Do not judge and measure yourself against the values of society, or of other people. What you are lies within. Know that you are the heart of a vast constellation of souls – a spiritual being within a human body, on a pilgrimage home.

Nurture your confidence through completion. Build your awareness of the good in your life. Attend to your deepest intuition. Listen to its quiet voice as that of a mentor and guide. Be willing to do whatever is needed to change inner knowledge into reality. Self-confidence comes forth from willingness as surely as a butterfly emerges from its cocoon.

What you can do, or
   dream you can, begin it.
Boldness has genius,
   power, and magic in it.
Only engage, and then
   the mind grows hearted.
Begin it, and the work
   will be completed.

JOHANN WOLFGANG VON GOETHE

EMPOWERING EXERCISE TO CHANGE NEGATIVE SELF-JUDGMENTS INTO POSITIVE EXPECTATIONS

First, identify your most positive qualities to affirm your goodness. Then, identify your least positive qualities and follow the treatment for change below. Add your own qualities to the list if they do not appear here.

1 **Most Positive Qualities**. List up to 10 qualities that most cause you to love and respect yourself.

Balanced	Intelligent
Calm	Joyous
Caring	Loyal
Cheerful	Moral
Determined	Open
Energetic	Persevering
Flexible	Playful
Generous	Polite
Gentle	Reliable
Grateful	Reverent
Helpful	Sympathetic
Honest	Trustworthy

....

....

....

....

....

2 **Least Positive Qualities**. List up to 10 qualities that cause you to not love and respect yourself.

Apathetic	Immoral
Arrogant	Jealous
Bitter	Lazy
Boastful	Lustful
Complaining	Pessimistic
Disorganized	Quarrelsome
Envious	Resentful
Fearful	Rude
Gossipy	Selfish
Greedy	Spiteful
Grudging	Unfaithful
Hostile	Violent

....

....

....

....

....

3 **Replace Negative Self-judgment with Lovingkindness**. The 2 steps that follow will help you to replace negative perceptions of yourself with feelings of worthiness, and with lovingkindness towards yourself. Use both steps each and every morning, for as long as you need to.

Write out this exact statement for each one of your negative qualities. *I love and respect myself **while** being* (insert negative quality), *and **while** taking positive steps to change.*

Recite the Serenity Prayer (page 123) in front of a mirror. Then, read each written statement out loud. Recite the Serenity Prayer again.

4 **Einstein Energy Diet, Enjoyable Exercise, Meditation, De-addiction**. Review these steps of the Pyramid of Human Aspiration, and reaffirm your resolve to strive towards balance in your body, mind, and spirit.

THREE STAGES OF LIFE

STAGE ONE – STARTING OUT
The magnificent Monarch butterfly pictured below starts life as an earthbound caterpillar. Its development follows the plan of nature.

STAGE TWO – TIME OF CHANGE
A chrysalis nurtures the caterpillar's internal change, just as human growth is nurtured by the constellation of souls that surrounds you.

STAGE THREE – SOARING ALOFT
When the butterfly emerges from its protective case, the process is complete – an earthbound creature is transformed into one that soars. In the same way, you too can soar aloft with the realization that your purpose in life is to help make something in this world perfect.

133

FINDING PURPOSE IN LIFE

WE ARE BORN not simply to eat, reproduce, thrill our senses, and then die. Human life is more precious and endowed with much greater meaning than that offered by mere existence. We are graced with a limitless capacity to appreciate Beauty, Love, and Truth. Thus, the purpose of all human life is to live each moment in the presence of these essences, to glorify them by ascending to the Good – your unchanging inner reality that is one with the universe, at its very heart and soul.

Discovering why you were brought into this world and why you exist and the unique purpose of your life is all revealed when you learn the truth about yourself.

Plato wrote a story about a cave, where human beings were shackled in such a way that they were forced to face its back wall forever. A fire burning behind them cast onto the wall the shadows of people walking in front of the cave's entrance. The inhabitants – unaware that people live outside of caves – believed the shadows to be real human beings.

In the same way, your senses define your reality. Being attached to one-dimensional surface images creates shadows of self-doubt born of desire and illusion. Thus, your senses can cloud your vision and dampen your energy, although your inner reality is truly *resplendent like a billion suns*.

ACTION WITH DIVINITY

Use the wise words above (from the *Bhagavad-Gita*, Song of the Blessed One) to find your purpose in life as you emerge from the shadowy cave of self-doubt into the light of truth.

In seeking what is true and real, be aware of nature's truth. Throughout the changing scenes of life, all your reactions and responses, this truth endures – *we reap what we sow*.

Plants and animals follow their instinct, emerging, maturing, and returning to the earth according to the laws of nature. So too does the celestial balance of nature ensure your fulfillment and joy, even as it orders the seasons. When a sense of sacredness governs your conduct, you are in concert with nature, and your true purpose becomes clear.

The greatest human quest is to know

what one must do

in order to become a human being.

IMMANUEL KANT

LIVING TRUTH & REALITY

Again, renew your faith in your self as a spiritual being having a human experience. How you care for your self, how well you live according to your whole nature, determines the quality of your pilgrimage home.

Each individual finds their own special purpose in life by infusing it with forgiveness and love. Develop patience. Fear not. View change as challenge. Light despondency with attainable hopes and dreams. Make choices that heal rather than hurt. Nurture your constellation of souls.

Above all, make Beauty, Love, and Truth the wellspring of your life. In many ways we seek to disprove that *man is as divine as nature, as infinite as the void*, yet the Ideal of *the Good* remains. Let faith in your goodness determine the conduct of your life.

These words of the poet, Goethe, give solace and hope as you reach the sixth step of the pyramid: *What you can do, or dream you can, begin it ... Boldness has genius, power, and magic in it ... Only engage, and then the mind grows hearted ... Begin it, and the work will be completed.*

EMPOWERING EXERCISE TO DEVELOP RESOLVE

Affirm your work in Step Five by responding to these questions.

- What sheds light on your gloom? *Rather light a candle than complain about darkness.* A CHINESE PROVERB
- Do you nurture other souls, and thus nurture yourself? *My religion is very simple. It is the religion of kindness.* THE DALAI LAMA
- What do you share with, or give away to, others? *Charity never faileth.* THE BIBLE
- What are you discovering to gain confidence, change, and develop? *The real voyage of discovery consists not in seeking new landscapes but in having new eyes.* MARCEL PROUST

REACHING FORGIVENESS

Forgiveness is heartfelt lovingkindness towards oneself and others that occurs with perceiving the sacredness of life. Forgiveness heals sorrows and wounds. Most people just want to be loved, appreciated, heard, and understood. Forgiving them does not mean tolerating injustice or acquiescing to hurt. Step Six identifies the sixth ideal – compassionate living in the here and now.

FORGIVENESS
SELF-ESTEEM
DE-ADDICTION
MEDITATION
ENJOYABLE EXERCISE
EINSTEIN ENERGY DIET

FORGIVENESS means creating an attitude of grace that allows you to relinquish past and present anger and hurt. Doing this does not make you vulnerable. Rather, forgiveness is the strength of the soul.

Love cannot exist where there is non-forgiveness. Not being able to forgive weakens the energy of body, mind, and spirit. Energy, needed to fight infections, overcome diseases, and support your life, is squandered in clinging to old hurts and angers, or in engaging with new ones.

If you set your mind and heart to turn from forgiveness, you just hurt yourself. Walls that you have raised keep love and peace at bay, casting deep shadows on life's sunnier side.

In attempts to bring sweetness into your life and prevent imprisonment, you may accumulate wealth, gather acquaintances, increase your scope of influence or power. Yet nothing can compensate for the oppression that crushes your heart and soul.

CLEARING THE PATH

Forgiveness tears down the walls of your prison. Willingness to forgive, and to be forgiven, can release you from mental bondage that has no greater strength to constrain than a hair holding a wild beast captive.

Being able to forgive often occurs gradually, over time. But why wait? You have nothing to lose, yet much to gain: your happiness and health.

The first five steps of the Pyramid of Human Aspiration have taught you that life's journey is a spiritual pilgrimage towards the Good. You know already that what is on your mind and in your heart *can* make you sick or keep you well.

Harboring disappointments and betrayals – refusing to let go of past hurt and pain – places obstacles on your path, boulders over which you must climb in order to move on.

Forgiveness clears your path. It sets you free from the past, so that you can live fully, with purpose, in the present. Reaching towards the summit of the Pyramid bathes you in the celestial light of truth where non-forgiveness cannot prevail.

REACHING FORGIVENESS – COMPASSIONATE LIVING IN THE PRESENT

RESOLVING CONFLICT
Emotional pain is readily overcome by inner peace and goodness. There is no better way to resolve conflict than to let the strength of your soul shine forth – see pp. 138–139.

HEALING INNER PAIN
It is only your ego that labors to defend and justify your right to stay offended and hurt. Why hold on to negative emotions that add nothing to life but pain? – see pp.140–141.

NEUTRALIZING FEAR
A restless, troubled mind cannot release you from fear. Only stillness of thought, realized during meditation and prayer, can neutralize the effects of fear – see pp.142–143.

BE HAPPY – NOT RIGHT

Your unwillingness to be happy is a potential source of illness. For your own sake, it is therefore much more important for you to be happy than for your ego to be right.

In resolving to be happy rather than to nurse hurt pride, you make a healing choice that will help you break free of the chains of the past. Making this choice does not mean compromising your integrity. Most of what upsets people is not of real importance. *Why didn't she call?* or *Why was he so late?* have very little significance in the grand scheme of life. In such matters, it is never the soul aspiring to be right, only the wounded ego. Spiteful words, bitter thoughts, and grudging acts become harbored in the body as knots that disrupt balance, impede the flow of life-energy – and create conditions under which illness thrives. They clog arteries, stiffen joints, tighten muscles, raise the pulse, burn into

HEALING THROUGH FORGIVENESS
Feelings such as anger and fear transform into bodily ills. Compassionate living in the present releases life-energy to heal your whole being.

ulcers, and grip the heart and soul. Your soul aspires only to love. *Why hurt yourself over matters that have nothing to do with its purpose?*

Peacefulness is your natural state. Any thing that assaults or denies it is against your nature. Hold fast to what matters in the present. Strive towards the ideal of forgiveness.

Grant that I may not so much seek
to be consoled, as to console …
to be loved, as to love.
For it is in giving that we receive,
And in forgiving that we are forgiven.

ST. FRANCIS OF ASSISI

RESOLVING CONFLICT

Do you know how hard it is to be unkind to someone who is only ever kind to you? Hurt feelings and angry thoughts are readily overcome by goodness. If someone treats you unkindly, pay close attention to your own inner peace. There is no better way to resolve conflict or hostility than to let the strength of your soul shine forth. If you invest energy proving yourself right, your vitality is drained. Moments of quietness help distinguish what is worth the pain of discord and what is not.

The people we tend to quarrel with most often, and most painfully, are our friends and loved ones – people to whom we look for comfort, care, and support, who are significant to us and essential for our well-being.

When conflict loosens bonds of intimacy, woven and nurtured over time, fear clutches at our heart. We feel outraged and exposed – foolish, perhaps disenchanted. Our sense of perspective deserts us, just when we yearn to hear its mediating voice.

Yet conflict – whether with people dear to us, or with people who play a minor role in our lives – takes on meaning only if we choose to judge the other person as *bad* or *wrong*.

FELLOW TRAVELERS

Instead, we can decide to recognize the *goodness* in the other person, in spite of what they may be saying or doing. We can just realize who this other person is – another soul, like us, treading the same path, striving to do their best while they journey home. This diffuses pain and allows us to see discord as sparks of mental fire, fueled by our ego's insisting on its right to be offended. Our faults, so often magnified in others, then emerge in the light of compassion, understanding, and love simply as the other side of our goodness.

Thus we learn from our hurts to reap the fruits of conflict so that we evolve through upsets and disputes into more loving human beings.

CHOOSE LIGHT – NOT HEAT

To continue rising up the Pyramid of Human Aspiration, you need to remove obstacles that hinder your ascent and impede your progress.

Conflict creates fire in the soul. In moments of emotional conflict, it is the *heat* of the fire that causes the ego to smolder and erupt into flame. But just as fire gives *light* as well as heat, so too does conflict. You can make light shine through the veils of illusion that cloud and dim your perception. This requires discipline and strength, but it also recharges your vitality and energy. Wise Krishnamurti said: *You must understand the whole of life, not just one little part of it. That is why you must read, that is why you must look at the skies – that is why you must sing and dance, write poems, suffer, and* understand, *for all that is life.*

SALUTATION TO THE SOUL

Because conflict frequently arises with those we love most, a special word is necessary about forgiving parents, and brothers and sisters.

At all times, keep in mind your connectedness to them. Recognize your belonging to them, and theirs to you. Remember that they are a part of your constellation of souls: *you are them and they are you.*

For your own sake, forgive those you love. Let their love for you fill your mind and heart. Imagine it, if you can find no loving memories.

Plant the seeds of understanding in your garden of compassion – let them grow strong. And in the heat of conflict, recall the word that is the essence of daily yoga practice: Namaste. *I salute the divinity in you.*

PERSPECTIVES ON CONFLICT

The French novelist and aviator, Antoine de Saint-Exupéry, wrote: *Life has taught us that love does not consist in gazing at each other, but in looking outward together in the same direction.* You can neutralize conflict in ways that bring you closer to other people and enable you to learn from hurt.

If your perspective is like this …	*neutralize conflict with this strategy*
If you are negative and judge other people as bad or wrong, you see their faults and imperfections in them, rather than what is good. Your mind and heart may begin to adopt attitudes that result in disaffection and neglect.	You can nurture the spirit of both unlovable people and those you love by encouraging their better points. Especially with children, praise is the verbal form of love. This strategy causes goodness to bloom and self-esteem to rise.
If you are confrontational and feel opposed to other people, you see potential for argument in every conflict. But arguing about who is right or who is to blame never ends a dispute, since one person is left shattered while the other feels guilty and misunderstood.	You can nurture respect for others by demonstrating your love and support for them at least once a day. Do not delay until a major difference of opinion forces you to declare the affection you feel. This strategy honors individuals as unique and special.
If you are self-righteous, then your ego already has you cornered. It is surely never the most reliable source to get you out of conflict. When arrogance begins or fuels conflict, the same behavior will not help release you from it.	You can nurture your true self and disarm your ego by trying to see what is ridiculous in everything. A sense of humor is the ultimate instrument to silence your ego. This strategy lightens your soul with laughter, joy, and relief.

Have you learned lessons from only those
who have admired you, and were tender
with you, and stood aside for you?
Have you not learned great lessons from those
who braced themselves against
you, and disputed the passage with you?

WALT WHITMAN

HEALING INNER PAIN

YOUR SOUL aspires only to love. It is just your ego that defends and justifies your inner pain. Only your ego wants you to hold on to negative emotions such as anger, guilt, and shame. For its very survival, it labors to defend and justify your right to go on being offended and hurt. *Why carry these negative emotions with you from the past? Why cling to them in the present?* Holding on to negative emotions is fruitless. They destroy the inner peace you seek, and add nothing to your life but pain.

When someone upsets you or hurts your feelings, it is the voice of your ego that attempts to convince you to hold on to your inner pain. But the voice of your soul tells you to forgive and let go of pain.

When you decide to not forgive, it is as if you are actively making a hurtful choice instead of a healing one. Withholding forgiveness from yourself – or from others – is never conducive to your health and well-being. Guilt, shame, and anger raise the specter of illness by obstructing the flow of your *healing force*.

Thus, to encourage the spirit of remembered wellness, it is far more important for you to be happy than it is for your ego to be right.

STOP HARMING YOURSELF

Forgiveness is the intrinsic nature of the human soul. Therefore, not forgiving yourself or others requires an active effort on your part to stay offended or hurt.

Holding on to harmful thoughts and emotions is felt as inner pain. Forgiveness allows you to heal that pain. Forgiving merely requires you to cease actively harming yourself, in spite of your ego's most stubborn efforts to justify how *right* you are. Whenever you give in to your ego's justifications for staying upset, you are just denying your true nature.

TIMING & STRATEGY

If you give in to your ego, you are not only denying your true nature. You are also destroying your sense of inner peace and calm. Your ego will even convince you that it has nothing to do with your upsetness. This process is called *denial*.

Ascending the Pyramid enables you to overcome denial. It requires both *timing* and *strategy*. You alone can decide *when* you are willing to get over what bothers you and *how long* it will take. The choice is in your hands – to prolong your pain and hurt, or to release yourself at once from your mental turmoil.

The *strategy* to overcome denial begins by reviewing the issues and conflicts you are harboring in your mind, and calmly evaluating them. Then you must disarm your ego and dismantle its mechanism by asking yourself three questions.

QUESTIONS TO HEAL PAIN

Answer these questions when you are relaxed, after yoga, walking, or meditation, since *truth* is glimpsed only through inner peace.
• Is the conflict you are holding on to truly about Goodness, Love, Truth, or Justice?
• Is withholding forgiveness for yourself or others more conducive to your happiness and inner peace than giving up your anger now?
• If your upsetness is at yourself, will you now declare your intention never to do again whatever you did that caused your anger? (see box)

As you ponder your responses to the three questions, keep this ideal clearly in your mind: *Forgiveness is never enough until it is complete.*

RELEASING ANGER

Your ego invents endless reasons for you to stay upset with yourself. However, you can help release guilt and shame by replacing these emotions with forgiveness and love.

1 List at least 5 things you feel guilty of or ashamed about.

....

....

....

....

2 Practice releasing your anger with the following 3 steps.
• Vow never to repeat this or any other kind of conduct that has caused you pain.
• Forgive yourself completely.
• Declare your firm intention by signing your name and adding the date below.

SIGNATURE
....

DATE
....

THE NEED TO CULTIVATE COMPASSION

At the very height of the Pyramid of Human Aspiration, you will discover that you can transform inner pain into compassion, which is the doorway to love. Then, the only thing still to forgive is a refusal to hear the sweet melody of Love that is the song of the soul.

To laugh often and much: to appreciate beauty: to find the best in others: to leave the world a bit better … To know even one life has breathed easier because you have lived: that is to have succeeded.

RALPH WALDO EMERSON

NEUTRALIZING FEAR

FEAR IS the grip of your past that prevents you from living fully and peacefully in the present. What you feel as fear is merely a response to your memories. When your memories evoke fear, what has happened in the past interferes with your life in the present and seriously affects your future. In this way, fear ties you to the past and eats away at your present health and future happiness. What is past is gone. *What is gone persists only in your mind.* Only in your mind can you neutralize your fear.

The instinctual response to danger is to feel fear. From the perspective of biology, fear is necessary for our protection from physical harm.

Yet in the world today, threats to our survival come disguised more as worry and fatigue than as wild and hungry beasts. Fear is no longer the appropriate response – indeed, most fear is simply an emotional illusion that has acquired a life of its own, over time. Using fearful thoughts to diminish fear is futile, because it is exactly these thoughts that created your fear in the first place.

However, just as your thoughts create fear, so you can quiet your thoughts in order to come into the present moment and create peace. You can replace a fearful, worried, or restless mind with a mind filled with only stillness and peace.

WHAT GIVES RISE TO FEAR?

If you are fearful and worried, it is because you have forgotten that the ultimate, and inexhaustible, source of your protection from danger lies within you. You have lost the sense of yourself as a spiritual being. It is no wonder that you feel unsafe and insecure. The future may bring you pain, or it may not – but if you fear the future now, you will already be suffering. Such was the realization of Montaigne when he cautioned: *He who fears he shall suffer, already suffers what he fears.*

You cannot neutralize fear with a restless, troubled mind. Attempts to analyze or escape fear with a fearful mind are no more successful than if you were trying to quench fire with fire. To relieve your mind of worry and memories that create fear, you must first still your thoughts. Only stillness of thought, realized during meditation and prayer, can release you from the bondage of your fears.

STRATEGIES TO DEAL WITH WORRY & FATIGUE

Fatigue creates apathy and anxiety. Worry generates fear. While you may not be able to control people and events, you *can* control your response to them. Ascending the Pyramid increases your perception of your ability to cope. If that perception is high, your levels of worry will be low.

At times when you feel like this …	*empower yourself with this strategy*
When your thoughts are overcome with worry that clouds the light of truth, remember that the act of worrying never helps. It just allows fear and anxiety to get a firmer grip. Worry is a product of your imagination, an illusion in which the future is mistaken for the present – nothing more.	You can remove the veil of illusion and come back into the present by stilling your thoughts through meditation. Meditating brings a sense of peace. Worry disappears in the stillness of your thoughts, enveloped by the healing powers of your own internal pharmacy.
When you feel tired or weary, any substance that robs energy will further disrupt your balance, in particular "quick fixes" such as alcohol, caffeine, nicotine, and candy. Make a special effort to avoid all these energy thieves.	You can dispel fatigue by balancing your energy through exercise and good nutrition. Pay attention to the Einstein Energy Diet, eating foods from the upper 5 rungs of the Ladder (page 59). Do yoga and wellness walking daily.

MOUNTAINS OF COURAGE
Fear breeds more fear, but living in the present moment, with compassion, instills mountains of courage. You free yourself from fear once you realize that, when your thoughts are still and the soul is calm, you cannot even feel its effect. Then you can gaze towards the summit of the Pyramid of Human Aspiration, where the bright light of love shines through fear.

The wise man in the storm prays God, not for safety
from danger, but for deliverance from fear. It is the storm
within that endangers him, not the storm without.

RALPH WALDO EMERSON

LIVING IN THE PRESENT

Fear is born in the mind, as are all other emotions. Freedom from fear requires the lifting of a veil from in front of your mind to perceive the truth that *the only thing you have to fear is fear itself*.

Fear and freedom *can* co-exist. It is when your ego becomes terrified of fear and tells you that there must be no fear that anxiety begins. The voice of your ego shouts: *Don't feel fear … don't show fear … don't admit to fear*. Thus, the greater your fear, the greater your resistance, and the greater the mental turmoil you feel.

The wonderful recognition that you can have emotions such as fear *and still control your response* releases you from your ego's grip. Then the experience of fear need never be so devastating or even uncomfortable.

You can begin, calmly, to observe your fear – admit it, accept it, and let it go without suffering its effect.

As you ascend the Pyramid, you are learning to live more and more in the here and now. In the present moment, there is no fear – because fear is merely the ties of the past or the pull of the future. Living in the present is living in balance and true harmony of body, mind, and spirit.

REDISCOVERING LOVE

LOVE
FORGIVENESS
SELF-ESTEEM
DE-ADDICTION
MEDITATION
ENJOYABLE EXERCISE
EINSTEIN ENERGY DIET

Forever true, forever beautiful, forever good – Love is the Ideal. Beneath illness lies a longing for love. Nothing affects health more deeply than love. Given freely, and without condition, love causes the soul to sing out. Give all to love, for the song of the soul is vital to bring balance and wellness into life. Step Seven identifies the seventh ideal – faith, conduct, and surrender.

EVEN WHEN you have lost touch with love, love still infuses your being – just as it infuses nature and the whole vastness of the universe. Love *is* all there is. It is the guiding principle, the cornerstone, and the very spirit of existence. Love is the universal theme in the magnificent symphony of life, reverberating in your heart, echoing everywhere.

By completing each of the fifteen questionnaires and assimilating the information in this book, you have been able to shine a spotlight into your mind and heart. Illuminating yourself thus has revealed the truth that what happens in your external life is a reflection of all you do and say, and of all you think and feel.

THE FINAL RESPONSIBILITY

Now you can see clearly where you are lacking love for yourself, or for others who are connected to you in your constellation of souls. Surely, you have learned where, and why, your energy is out of balance.

The seventh step of the Pyramid empowers you to take responsibility for making the ultimate change in your life. Your potential for healing and wellness depends on it.

You are ready to take this final step when you recognize that your attitudes, expectations, and beliefs trigger the mind–body connection that affects the countless chemical reactions occurring in each of your cells every moment you are alive.

Already, you have learned to care for your body as the safe haven for your soul, and to hold forgiveness in your mind and heart.

Love is the dimension that will inspire your conduct for the rest of your life. It ensures you unimpeded progress on life's journey. It sets the seal on a lifetime of wellness. But if you neglect your body, and harbor sadness in your mind, and close the door of your heart to love, then you make harmful choices that support discomfort and disease.

Love is the inner physician. It is healing energy more powerful than medicine. Love opens the door to your natural pharmacy that keeps you safe from illness and disease.

REDISCOVERING LOVE – FAITH, CONDUCT, & SURRENDER

TRANSCENDING ROMANTICISM
As long as there is desire, there is dissatisfaction – and thus worry, stress, and ill-health. True love is what endures – see pp.146–147.

RECOGNITION & TRUST
How is the mind prevented from casting its shadow over the soul, which alone knows the truth of love is all? – see pp.148–149.

SPIRITUAL WELLNESS
The ultimate spiritual effort is to strive always towards goodness, and to live by the ideal of loving one another – see pp.150–151.

RADICAL AMAZEMENT
At the summit of the Pyramid, the healing force resounds to the tuneful harmony of body, mind, and spirit – see pp.152–153.

LOVE THAT MOVES THE STARS
To rediscover love is to gaze upward to where the stars in the sky become angels in heaven, souls singing with joy, and bathing the whole universe with the sweet music of love – in the immortal words of Dante: the love that moves the sun and other stars.

WHAT BEING LOVING MEANS

You were born into this world as a loving being. Your soul craves love, languishes and grows faint in love's absence: you are meant to be loved. Giving and receiving love is what most influences your well-being.

Rediscovering love – for yourself and others – begins not with being loved, but with *being loving*. When you are being loving, your heart is transfixed, your soul is flooded with joy, every cell of your body radiates love, and the spirit of remembered wellness is revived. Then, the song of your soul is perfectly attuned and reverberates throughout your entire being, bringing balance, harmony, and reverence into your life.

For one human being to love another,
That is perhaps the most difficult of our tasks,
The ultimate, the last test and proof,
The work for which all other work is but preparation.

RAINER MARIA RILKE

TRANSCENDING ROMANTICISM

IN THE world of senses and possessions, nothing endures: everything disappears or dissolves. Yet this is the world that currently entertains so many individuals, and fuels their desires. Trying to find real meaning in this world is like trying to capture soap bubbles that constantly expand and burst. As long as there is desire, there will be dissatisfaction; as long as there is dissatisfaction, there is worry; as long as there is worry, there is stress and ill-health. All that we can trust is love. Love alone endures.

Your perception and understanding of love, as well as your beliefs and ideas about love, have been shaped over the years by many unconscious forces. Images of popular romance, unacknowledged desires, and past experiences of love lost or rejected all contribute to your view of love.

In addition, the ability to know, feel, and express true love has been hindered by the collective, popular consciousness of romanticism. The version of love that is the recurring theme of so many modern movies, songs, books, and magazines – and pervades so much of television and advertising – is not true love.

Instead, the version of love that is promoted today deals in illusion and images of hopelessly romantic myths – fairy tale romances, story-book weddings, perfectly modeled children, lavish gifts, incredible sex, and wonderful vacations.

WHY HOPES CRUMBLE

These media-driven myths seduce people into believing that they can depend on others to fulfill all their needs, and that happiness depends on finding Mr. or Mrs. Right. Such foolish hopes are prone to crumble and hopelessly romantic individuals are almost invariably disappointed. True love is never found in a bottle of expensive perfume or in a dream vacation on a tropical island. The meaning of true love is revealed in living each and every ordinary day with a loving heart.

A PURER FORM OF LOVE

Thus we can distinguish between popular ideas of love, and love in its purest human form. Such love is a feeling of inner contentment and security. Part of this feeling derives from the joyful memory of warmth and safety provided by people who cared for you at the very beginning of your life. However, in adult life, feelings that were appropriate as a child need also to mature, lest they grow into self-centered love, which is love given to others only because you expect love in return.

Mature love is based on valuing yourself and loving in a giving way. Therefore, rediscovering true love, for yourself and others, begins not with *being loved* but by *being loving*.

AFFECTION & FRIENDSHIP

Hurt and disappointment from the past may lead to your barricading yourself from love. Just the *thought* of being close to other people may stir discomfort and apprehension because of your perceived need to avoid pain – the pain of losing the person you love, or of having your love either ridiculed or rejected.

Sunshine was he

In the winter day;

And in the midsummer

Coolness and shade.

AN ARABIAN POET

If you have experienced hurt, and fear the closeness and intimacy of a loving relationship, it is particularly important to nurture a sense of self-value by living up to your highest potential. Review your progress in *Building Self-esteem* (pages 126–135) and recall that *affection, friendship, goodness,* and *kindness* are the most effective ways to heal inner pain.

The joy of sharing friendship and affection is a special inspiration to wellness – yet humility and a sense of humor are almost always needed. The philosopher, poet, and essayist, Ralph Waldo Emerson, addressed a dear friend in this way:

If I was sure of thee, sure of thy capacity, sure to match my mood with thine, I should never think again of trifles, in relation to thy comings and goings. I am not very wise: my moods are quite attainable … yet dare I not presume in thee a perfect intelligence of me and so thou art to me a delicious torment. Thine ever, or never.

LOVE FREELY GIVEN

Recognizing that it is the quality of your love that matters most enables you to complete your ascent of the Pyramid. Unconditional love is the aim: love offered selflessly, without expectation of anything in return.

This is not hopelessly romantic love. It is a deeper, unchanging yet ever-expanding love, love for love's sake, compassionate, flowing freely from the soul. When you give love freely in this way, your *healing force* is empowered because the love you give is reflected back to you. Then, your inner song and smile resound throughout your entire being, and your work on earth truly begins.

EMPOWERING EXERCISE TO TRANSFORM YESTERDAY'S SCARS INTO GLITTERING STARS

Hopeless romantics have difficulty building solid relationships because they dwell on what is past. If you harbor hurts, you cannot find peace. Stubbornness is the language of the ego: the soul speaks of forgiveness and love. You can dismantle barricades of past hurts by recognizing the good in others and just accepting them as souls on *their* journey home.

1 List 5 memories you have of feeling unloved or rejected.

2 Meditation is the most direct way to turn scars into stars. Therefore, during the next 5 days, after you have finished meditating, reflect upon each of the above 5 memories. Then, write down the positive aspects or outcomes of each event on 5 separate pieces of paper.

3 Wouldn't it be wonderful if there were a time you could recall every dear friend you ever made; every heart you ever touched; and every love you ever shared? *Let this be.* Write out all their names. Reflect upon each in turn. Consider collecting mementos of these loving relationships in an album or treasure box.

4 Write a poem or letter expressing your affectionate or loving feelings to someone who is a significant part of your life. It need not be great poetry – just what comes from your heart. If you wish, you can recite your poem to the person or mail it to them. If your poem or letter is to a special loved one, you might like to put it in a place where they can find it, unexpectedly. This is a particularly loving thing to do if you are – or have been – in conflict with them.

Like a summer day
Full of sunshine and flowers,
That's how you are like
And shall always be.

A PERSONAL LOVE POEM

147

RECOGNITION & TRUST

BEYOND THE world of the senses, there exists another world. There, immutable and eternal ideals reign, time without end. This is the reality of the Tao, Nature, God – and of the Good. The human heart knows both what is veiled from the mind, and what the mind forgets. By taking the last of these seven integral steps to self-healing, you are empowered to part the veils. Then, you can perceive, or be reminded of, these timeless truths and see the brilliance of their light again.

You are approaching the summit of the Pyramid of Human Aspiration. Through lessons learned from the previous six steps, you are already demonstrating an outstanding level of personal responsibility, building awareness of your own worthiness for love, and developing reverence for life. Now it is necessary to have flawless love in your heart in order to complete the ascent to *the Good*. Let this timeless wisdom be your comfort and guide: *Fear not.*

SHADOWS CAST BY THE MIND

The universe, as we know it, began when a flicker of light, infused with Love, burst into matter. Everything that has life was created from this tiny spark of energy.

Your *healing force*, which revives the spirit of *remembered wellness*, is concentrated in the powerful energy system that is your body. Your very life is thus part of all that ever was, and of everything that exists.

You feel this connectedness in the calmness of your mind and the stillness of your soul that occurs in meditation. But how is it possible to comprehend that you are energy suspended in time and space, just like stardust? How can you prevent your intellect from casting mental shadows over the light of your soul? How can you grasp that *love is all?*

The soul is made of the … substance of redeemed energy,
energy that has returned to the Source of all
energy through man, through the alchemy of the heart.

RESHAD FEILD

LOVE INFUSES ALL

Only through intuitive *recognition* and *trust* can you grasp the reality that love is, and infuses, all. These words of mathematician, physicist, and philosopher, Blaise Pascal, can give you guidance: *It is the heart that experiences God, and not reason.*

Once you disregard the fact that *nothing in life happens by chance*, you are faced with the dilemma that is uniquely human. You *are* a spiritual being having a human experience. Your life *is* a pilgrimage back to the Source of all. During your journey, what you reap depends on how and what you sow. You experience life as a series of consequences that are reflections of what you think, what you feel, and what you do.

THE DANCE OF DUALITIES

Therefore, *luck* has little to do with what happens to us, in spite of how most people view their lives. Even when seemingly bad things happen to good people, there is opportunity for growth in overcoming difficulty.

Our spiritual sense deepens and matures when we realize that forces we once thought of as opposing are also complementary. This brings all aspects of our life into sharper focus and a meaningful pattern emerges. Then, life runs more smoothly, and there is only the timeless, inspired moment of perception – that life *is* the dance of dualities that reunites good and not good, happiness and sorrow, and darkness and light.

NO SHADOWS OF DOUBT

Without inner love, the love of the soul, outward love is formless. Each of the steps to self-healing has been designed, therefore, to enable you to follow your soul's impulse to be loving. If you still feel badly about past events, return to the *forgiveness step*, review your incompleted work, and recommit. So, too, review your work with the other steps: *nutrition, exercise, meditation, de-addiction, and self-esteem.* If you have arrived at this point carrying heavy baggage, your ascent will be incomplete.

Reaching now higher brings the reward of *faith*: the recognition that all life is sacred; knowing you have a special mission; believing you are divinely guided. Love *is* all there is. With faith in this truth held steady in your heart, your mind casts no shadows of doubt. At the summit, the sun lies over your head, where no shadows fall, and none are cast.

I AM WITH YOU & YOU ARE MINE

A woman, in the saddest time of her life, walked across a beach, all the while crying aloud to God to walk beside her. Then, falling into a deep sleep, she dreamed of many scenes of her life in which two sets of footprints appeared in the sand. In each scene, one set was always hers, while the other was God's.

Upon awakening, she could see only a single set of footprints, and began to wonder if God had forsaken her. Then, in her meditation, God spoke with her to bring solace, and said: *My precious child, the reason you see only one set of footprints is because I was carrying you all the while. Wherever you are, I am with you and you are mine.*

Once you discover the truth, that all life is sacred, and that your life is guided by a divine spirit, you realize that you are never alone. In meditation, your burdens will ease as you surrender and just let God help bear your pain.

SPIRITUAL WELLNESS

THE PRESENCE of God is everywhere. It infuses every living thing. With this truth comes the recognition of ourselves as spiritual beings having a human experience. Spiritual energy reawakens our mental and physical energy. Then, we become invested with meaning and purpose: to be loving towards all and to strive always towards goodness. When spiritual energy soars in graceful harmony with the energy of body and mind, all turbulence dissolves and the *healing force* is at last unleashed.

Wellness is the eternally unfolding dance of human life, in which the energy of body, mind, and spirit is perfectly attuned. At this point of balance, the power of your *healing force* can flow freely to nurture and nourish your whole being.

Your *healing force* becomes ever stronger as your eyes are opened to see that your wellness flowers when it is watered by the gentle dews of personal responsibility, self-value, and reverence for life.

Seeing and perceiving that every atom of your being is infused with meaning endows your *healing force* with its strongest source of power. This meaning is manifested in your conscious daily acts of being loving and extolling the divinity of nature. Thus, all human beings are meant to aspire to *the Good*: truth, beauty, goodness, and love.

LOVE ONE ANOTHER

Plato, a philosopher, defined God as *the Good*. Aristotle, his student and a scientist, studied every form of physical life, and concluded that all contain a spark of divinity. The vastness of divinity transcends our limited comprehension. God works through unknown and subtle ways to create solar systems, change the course of destiny, cast mountains into the sea, and breathe life into every thing. Therefore, *divine love* is the inner reality and essence of every living thing. The world that we know is merely a veil which, if removed, reveals divinity. *Love one another* is the unifying theme of all traditional faiths. To live this ideal, to strive always towards goodness, is the ultimate spiritual effort.

THE VIEW BEYOND

Helping to make something in life perfect is our mission. We can do this simply by *loving one another*.

More than ever, the world needs you to live by this ideal, and fulfill your mission. When enough people have sufficient love in their hearts, a chain reaction will inspire a new *era of enlightenment* in which peace on earth finally prevails.

SPIRITUAL FAITH

Divine love is the whole reason for our existence – it is the underlying principle of all life. When you have *faith* and trust in this principle, you know that you are never burdened with more than you can bear. So, if you take one heartfelt step towards God, God takes one thousand steps towards you. If you cry one genuine heartfelt tear, God wipes away one thousand of your tears.

SPIRITUAL CONDUCT

Beliefs are not spiritual unless they are manifested in spiritual *conduct*. Therefore, make ethics a barometer for your behavior. Let the whisper of your heart be the voice of truth and the motivation for good action.

SPIRITUAL SURRENDER

The meditations in this book guide you to *surrender* to divine qualities already within you. As this is done, and as you strive towards the Good, "I and mine" gives way to thoughts of "thee and thine." Then the door of your heart is opened to the final surrender – the unfailing certainty that nothing in the changing world can do you any harm, once you are able to proclaim: *Thy will be done*.

PREVENTIVE THEOLOGY – ARTICLES OF FAITH

Paramahansa Yogananda, a great Indian sage, said that *with the dawn of spiritual ambition, we choose a chisel of wisdom to mold our life.* Spend time contemplating the articles of faith enshrined in the ten quotations here. As your chisel, use this powerful four-sentence affirmation of American theologian, Robert H. Schuller: I AM. I CAN. I WILL. I BELIEVE.

ARTICLE I
The unexamined life is not worth living. PLATO

ARTICLE II
We are what we repeatedly do. Excellence, then, is not an act, but a habit. ARISTOTLE

ARTICLE III
Love is the beginning and end, the alpha and omega of existence. ETHICS OF JUDAISM

ARTICLE IV
Behind every blade of grass is its very own angel that forever whispers: grow … grow. ETHICS OF JUDAISM

ARTICLE V
The most beautiful thing a person can do is to forgive wrong. ETHICS OF JUDAISM

ARTICLE VI
Seek and you shall find. Ask and it shall be given. Knock and it shall be opened unto you. TENETS OF CHRISTIANITY

ARTICLE VII
Let not the sun go down on your wrath. TENETS OF CHRISTIANITY

ARTICLE VIII
Animosity does not eradicate animosity. Only by loving-kindness is animosity dissolved. BUDDHIST PSALM

ARTICLE IX
Wherever you look, there is the face of God. KORAN

ARTICLE X
Start the day with love. Fill the day with love. End the day with love. SATHYA SAI BABA

My God, my God,

I pray that these things never end:

The sand and the sea, the rush of waters,

The lightening of the heavens,

The prayer of the soul.

HANNAH SENESH

RADICAL AMAZEMENT

YOUR ASCENT to *the Good* has taken you on a journey inward as well as upward, to glimpse the *Absolute and Infinite* that is the source of life. Goodness is the truth and beauty of your soul. It is the inner voice of love that guides you onward.

Radical amazement is your awakened knowledge of life's immensity. The awe that such knowledge inspires places you at the threshold of wisdom and the dawning of reverence for life. Healing, begun deep within you, now expands in the light of love.

The Pyramid of Human Aspiration is where divinity touches the earth. At its summit, you are gripped with awe and overcome by the sure and certain knowledge of God's love.

Here at the point of balance, you understand at last that the energy coursing through your whole being is the same energy that permeates the whole of Nature. Now, you are living life in full accord with what you have learned in rising through each of the seven steps. Your mind is calm. Fear is cast out. A chord is touched that merges all the energy of your body, mind, and spirit into one tuneful harmony, making your *healing force* resound and soar, and setting your inner compass directly towards *remembered wellness*.

Rediscovering love is your own epiphany. Journey on now, gazing ever upwards to where the stars in the sky become angels in heaven, souls singing with joy, bathing the sky with the music of love: *the love that moves the sun and other stars*.

PERSONAL PLEDGE FOR LIFE

I vow to use the gifts of my mind and my heart to do the very best
I can. To treat my body as a haven for my soul, to unleash the
infinite power of my Healing Force, and to encourage
my eternal spirit of Remembered Wellness.

SIGNATURE
_____

DATE
_____

UNCONDITIONAL
LOVE KNOWS
NO CONSTRAINTS

•

IT IS THE MOST
POWERFUL
HEALER OF ALL

•

LIVE EACH MOMENT
OF LIFE IN
THE LIGHT OF LOVE

RESOURCES FOR HEALING

The Selected Writings of Ralph Waldo Emerson edited by Brooks Atkinson. The Modern Library, New York, New York 1992. *Essayist, philosopher, and poet, Emerson reminds us that if we live truly, we see truly.*

Timeless Healing by Herbert Benson, M.D. Scribner, New York, New York 1996. *A respected Harvard physician supplies hundreds of scientific references to support his belief that up to ninety per cent of our illnesses are curable through Remembered Wellness.*

I and Thou by Martin Buber. Scribner, New York, New York 1958. *This classic work by a Jewish philosopher explains God's presence everywhere. It becomes an enlightened poem that blurs the distinctions between all religions of love.*

A Dancing Star by Eileen Campbell. Aquarian Press, London 1991. *A treasury of inspired quotations from East and West.*

The Encyclopedia of Medicinal Plants by Andrew Chevallier. DK Publishing, New York, New York 1996. *A comprehensive, practical, fully illustrated reference for anyone who wishes to learn about or use herbal medicine.*

Ageless Body, Timeless Mind by Deepak Chopra, M.D. Harmony, New York, New York 1993. *A noted physician offers breathtaking truths derived from both Ayurvedic Medicine and quantum physics to inspire mind, body, and spirit.*

Descartes' Error by Antonio Damasio, M.D. Grosset/Putnam, New York, New York 1994. *One of the world's foremost neurologists presents a revolutionary portrait of how body, mind, and soul interact always as an ensemble.*

Fit For Life by Harvey and Marilyn Diamond. Warner, New York, New York 1985. *This uniquely popular nutrition book offers good sense for healthful living and weight control.*

Your Sacred Self by Wayne Dyer, PH.D. HarperCollins, New York, New York 1991. *A clear dissection of the human ego that offers valuable psychological insight.*

The Alchemy of the Heart by Reshad Feild. Element Books Ltd., Shaftesbury, Dorset 1990. *The author emphasizes that if our world is to endure, it must be built on love.*

Man's Search For Meaning by Victor E. Frankl, M.D. Washington Square Press, New York, New York 1959. *This psychiatrist survived a concentration camp with unwavering faith by never doubting where God was. Instead, he asks this heartbreaking question: Where was man?*

Sophie's World by Jostein Gaarder. Ferrar, Straus and Giroux, New York, New York 1994. *In this delightful book, the author explains philosophy to her young daughter, and makes Socrates, Plato, Aristotle, and others come alive.*

Siddhartha by Hermann Hesse. Bantam, New York, New York 1951. *A rich, colorful, and sensitively written novel that explores the life and teachings of The Buddha. This inspired book is a timeless classic that lingers in the mind and spirit.*

Origins of Consciousness in the Breakdown of the Bicameral Mind by Julian Jaynes. Penguin Books Ltd., London 1979. *In this powerful achievement, the author explains how our consciousness (the human capacity to look inward) became an outgrowth of a huge historical neurosis.*

The Flame of Attention by J. Krishnamurti. Harper and Row, New York, New York 1984. *This Indian scholar reminds us that observation is like a flame of attention. With the capacity of observation, wounds and feelings of hurt and hate are burned away and gone for all time.*

Five Weeks To Healing Stress by Valerie O'Hara, PH.D. New Harbinger, Oakland, California 1996. *Here is an enjoyable and effective stress reduction program – a modern, therapeutic approach to the ageless science of yoga, written by an eminent yoga teacher.*

Mind as Healer, Mind as Slayer by Kenneth Pellitier, PH.D. Delacorte, New York, New York 1977. *A brilliant explanation of how we stay well or why we become sick, this work clearly and scientifically sets the stage for the entire field of psychoneuroimmunology.*

Sai Baba the Holy Man, and the Psychiatrist by Samuel Sandweiss, M.D. Birth Day Publishing, San Diego, California 1975. *With great sensitivity, a respected physician explores his profound spiritual transformation after meeting an avatar. An inspirational document of human possibility.*

Self-Esteem: The New Reformation by Robert H. Schuller. Word Books, Waco, Texas 1982. *An eminent theologian weaves history and psychology together to offer individual redemption through Christ-centered Christianity based on charity and lovingkindness.*

Love, Medicine & Miracles by Bernie S. Siegel, M.D. HarperCollins, New York, New York 1986. *This cancer surgeon offers touching wisdom for healing by sharing the hopes and dreams of his exceptional patients who refused to give up hope or to stop dreaming.*

Man's Presumptuous Brain by A.T.W. Simeons, M.D. E.P. Dutton, New York, New York 1960. *A groundbreaking explanation of how disease develops as a result of the unceasing struggle between the thinking part of the brain and the instinctual part of the brain.*

Prescription For Life by Edward Taub, M.D. Wellness Medicine Institute, Dana Point, California 1988. *"A work of extraordinary merit. An up-to-date guide in putting the patient's own resources to work" – Norman Cousins.*

The Wellness Rx by Edward Taub, M.D. Prentice Hall, Englewood Cliffs, New Jersey 1995. *"An intelligent, sensitive guide for a fuller, healthier life. Read it for direction on life's journey" – Bernie Siegel, M.D.*

The Yellow Emperor's Classic of Internal Medicine translated by Ilza Veith. University of California Press, Berkeley, California 1949. *This beautiful book is the oldest document in Chinese Medicine. It is a landmark in the history of Chinese culture and essential reading for all serious health care professionals.*

The Bhagavad Gita – A New Translation by Paramahansa Yogananda. Self Realization Fellowship, Los Angeles, California 1995. *A modern spiritual master has bequeathed a great truth to humanity in this stunning new version of India's immortal dialogue between soul and spirit.*

SPECIAL RESOURCES
Seven Steps to Self-Healing Seminars by Edward Taub, M.D. *For information on seminars, other programs, and educational materials, please contact The Wellness Medicine Institute, P.O. Box 4131, Dana Point, California 92629. Phone 800–720–9355.*

INDEX

159

ACKNOWLEDGMENTS

AUTHOR'S ACKNOWLEDGMENTS

I would like to express my gratitude to the following people. Anneli, my wife and *b'sherte*, created a peaceful nest to help me build self-esteem, reach forgiveness, and rediscover love. She also inspired the Einstein Energy Diet, contributed most of its recipes, and made dining into a spiritual experience. *Namaste*, Anneli. Lora Taub, Ph.D., my daughter, contributed her brilliance, lovingkindness, and communications skills. Marc Taub, M.D., my son, inspired me with his nobility and excellence as a physician. Lanny Taub, M.D., my brother and friend, was always there. Sue Myers helped me to develop the Wellness Energy Profile. Ron Myers, John Crane, Tim Standish, Mike Craig, Phil Gower, and Valerie and Brian O'Hara offered professional insight and assistance. Daniel and Roslyn, my parents, always demonstrated that love is all there is. Rabbi Abraham Heschel perceived of *Radical Amazement*, Dr. Robert H. Schuller conceived of *Preventive Theology*, and Dr. Herbert Benson invoked *Remembered Wellness*. Muriel Nellis, my literary agent, provided friendship and encouragement, and became my mentor. Norman Cousins and Dr. Jonas Salk gave me passion to persevere.

I am grateful to my friends and colleagues at Dorling Kindersley, who helped focus my thirty years of clinical experience into a lyrical vision. Peter Kindersley and Christopher Davis first envisioned this book, then oversaw the transformation of that vision into reality. For creating and sustaining a synergistic combination of aesthetic beauty and professional excellence at Dorling Kindersley, they will always have my deepest gratitude. Gillian Roberts, my editor, steadfastly nurtured, inspired, and strengthened this book from conception to completion, with enormous effort, unwavering faith, and unshakable integrity. Bill Mason, my art editor, critically evaluated each of my ideas in the light of his keen intelligence and vast experience, and converted my dreams into a beautiful picture. Mary-Clare Jerram and Amanda Lunn gently yet firmly directed my efforts while offering encouragement and goodwill. Jeanette Mall and Connie Robinson at DK Publishing offered focus and guidance.

COMMISSIONED PICTURE CREDITS

Food photography on pages 60 to 75 by Clive Streeter, assisted by Andy Whitfield. Yoga, Wellness Walking, & Meditation photography on pages 82 to 99 by Steve Gorton, assisted by Sarah Ashun. Author photograph by Greg Figge at Figge Studios. These and all other photographs, except those detailed under agency picture credits at right, copyright © 1996 Dorling Kindersley Limited, London. Spiral artworks on pages 12 & 15 by Janos Marffy. Tree artwork on page 11 by Sue Oldfield.

PUBLISHER'S ACKNOWLEDGMENTS

Grateful thanks to the following people for their essential contributions to this book. Mark Bracey gave DTP support; Margaret Cornell prepared the index; Murdo Culver, Helen Robson, and Robert Campbell provided design assistance; Claudine Edwards and Rebecca Davies transcribed the eight meditations; Jill Eggleton tested, recreated, and wrote the recipes; Emma Jane Frost prepared food for photography; Karen Gibilaro, make-up artist, assisted the model during photography; Barbara Harding lent her instructor's critical eye to the yoga photography; Jo Harvey was the perfect model for the yoga, walking, and meditation photography; Emily Hedges gave sensitive help with picture research; Isobel Holland saved the editorial day; Norma MacMillan edited the recipes; Lesley Malkin provided a boost of editorial energy; Noah Health Food Stores offered helpful advice on grains and legumes; Ann Price analyzed the recipes for their nutritional content; John Stevenson sourced additional picture material; the Theatrical Hosiery Company created the yoga costume.

Heartfelt thanks to Bill Mason for inspiring much laughter & for his rendering of the twenty-third psalm. A special debt of gratitude is due to Melville P. Roberts, M.D., William Beecher Scoville Professor of Neurosurgery, University of Connecticut School of Medicine, Farmington, CT. for kind advice & for setting his compass ever towards Albion.

AGENCY PICTURE CREDITS

The publisher would like to thank the following sources for their kind permission to reproduce the photographs in this book. **Bridgeman Art Library/British Museum, London** 11 *above center*, **/National Museum of India, New Delhi** 11 *top right*, **/Oriental Museum, Durham University** 20 *top left*, **/Vatican Museums and Art Galleries** 10 *top left & above center*. **Bruce Coleman** 53 *above & below center*, 115, 131. **ET Archive** 10 *below center*. **Michael Holford** 16 *right of center*, 53 *top right*. **The Hulton Deutsch Collection** 11 *right of center*. **Images Colour Library** 1, 2–3, 6, 8–9, 13 *right of center & bottom*, 15 *bottom*, 22–23, 24 *left & center*, 25, 26, 32, 44 *left & right*, 46, 48–49, 50 *left & right*, 51 *center*, 53 *center*, 54, 101, 103, 107, 109, 113, 115, 116 *left, center, & right*, 117, 123, 124, 126 *right*, 133 *top, center, & bottom*, 134–135, 136 *left & right*, 137, 138, 143, 144 *left, left and right of center, & right*, 145, 146, 148, 149, 150, 152–153, 155, 160. **Impact Photos/Alan Evrard** 16 *left of center*, 18. **Scala** 10 *bottom*, 14 *top*. **Science Photo Library** 16 *bottom left*, 17 *top right*, 126 *left of center*, 130, **/Mehan/Kulyk** 16 *bottom right*, 20 *bottom right*. **Tony Stone Images** 5, 38, 45 *left*, 51 *right*, 52, 105, 111, 126 *left & right of center*, 127, 128, 132, 136 *center*, 140, 141.